PIGS FOR THE FREEZER

A GUIDE TO SMALL-SCALE PRODUCTION

PIGS FOR THE FREEZER

A GUIDE TO SMALL-SCALE PRODUCTION

LINDA MCDONALD-BROWN

THE CROWOOD PRESS

First published in 2010 by
The Crowood Press Ltd
Ramsbury, Marlborough
Wiltshire SN8 2HR

www.crowood.com

British Library Cataloguing-in-Publication Data
A catalogue record for this book is available from the British Library.

ISBN 978 1 84797 162 3

Disclaimer
The author and the publisher do not accept any responsibility in any manner whatsoever for any error or omission, or any loss, damage, injury, adverse outcome, or liability of any kind incurred as a result of the use of any of the information contained in this book, or reliance upon it. If in doubt about any aspect of keeping pigs readers are advised to seek professional advice.

Typeset by Servis Filmsetting Ltd, Stockport, Cheshire

Printed and bound in Malaysia by Times Offset (M) Sdn Bhd

Contents

Acknowledgements

There are so many people I want to thank, but three in particular have been of great help and given me valued support over the few months that I have been researching and writing this book. Many thanks to Tracey Jaine and her wonderful Mangalitza (a breed of which we bought two). Prior to the writing of this book, I did not know Tracey, she has become my sort of person and a good friend. I just wish she lived closer! I also want to thank Pauline Shannon, who has been a good friend and a fantastic support. Does that girl ever run out of patience? Thanks also to Carolyn Wheatley Hubbard from The Ginger Piggery, who sent me many meat photographs taken during her butchery courses, and who has been so incredibly helpful.

Finally, I would like to thank all the people who have willingly giving me photographs and information: Marcus Bates of the British Pig Association, Chris Neath of Panarama Welsh Pigs, John and Mary Weakes, Pippa Carpenter Knight, Elma McLaren from Ballencrieff Rare Pedigree Pigs and Farmshop, Ian and Maggie Todd, Smallicombe Herd of Pedigree Pigs. Michele Baldock, Anne from Emma's Pigs, Nikki at Ardross Farm, Lillian Waddell, Lisa Kennedy at Tatton Park, M. J. Kiddy & Son, Solitaire Farm, Gamlingay, Bedfordshire, Debbie Dawson from Hidden Valley Pigs, Rosemary Mills, Shirley Bowring, Wendy Scudamore from Barton Hill Kune Kunes, Heather Royal and the Oxford Sandy and Black Club, Brian Peacock, Frank Millar and the British Lop Pig Society, Maria Day, Silvy Weatherall, New Cample Farmshop, and, last but not least, Sue Fildes and her wonderful Dittisham Herd pigs.

I would also like to dedicate this book to my two young sons Harry and Hamish, who one day, I hope, will keep a couple of pigs for the freezer.

CHAPTER 1

The Pig – A Source of Food

KEEPING PIGS

Never has there been an animal that has played such an important and intricate part in the life of our ancestors as the pig, yet has been so misjudged and abused. Our unique relationship with these fantastic animals goes back as far as Neolithic times, when they provided early hunter/gatherer man with much-needed meat. Cave paintings thousands of years old, showing the special relationship that existed between man and pig, have been found in Europe, whilst in England pig's remains have been found at Neolithic sites.

Initially it was the old and the sick pigs that were captured and eaten, but, as the human population increased and demand for meat grew, ways had to be devised of containing the pigs so that they could be captured more easily when needed.

Over time, as basic farming of pigs progressed and tastes evolved, selective breeding began; it had become clear that pigs were developing in different ways, depending on the part of the country and the environment in which they lived. Some pigs, for example, were longer and leaner, whilst others yielded a higher percentage of fat. The Romans very early on recognized the benefits of selective breeding and improved their pig keeping to such an extent that pork production was spread across their empire.

Through the ages, man's relationship with the pig strengthened until the animal became firmly embedded in his day-to-day life, although it was not always kept in the most favourable conditions. Most rural households had pigs, providing them with a cheap source of food, but living in a city or town did not stop small-scale producers from flourishing either. Hundreds of pigs were kept in the back allies of slums, providing the poor neighbourhoods with a never-ending supply of pork. Sometimes, it was impossible to walk more than a few feet between makeshift pigsties. In medieval times, Paris had so many pigs available for slaughter that pork became the cheapest meat. From the mid-nineteenth century, however, the practice of keeping pigs in an urban setting started to decline quite dramatically. Towns and cities were experiencing a population explosion and the authorities, desperate to clean up their streets, introduced rules and regulations that made it more difficult for urban households to keep pigs.

During the Second World War, the practice of households keeping pigs was once again revived in Britain. Indeed, it was encouraged by the government, in the belief that it would make a valuable contribution towards the country's meat supply. There was an acute grain shortage, so the authorities also had to look at ways of reducing the grain rations fed

MR. G. M. ALLENDER'S TAMWORTH PIG.

The Tamworth is the closest relative of the wild boar.

to pigs and substituting them with other foodstuffs.

In 1940, the Small Pig Keepers Council was set up, actively to promote traditional self-sufficiency practices. Scrap-food collections were set up and posters encouraged people to feed pigs on the waste food from kitchens, gardens and allotments. Incentives were given to families who practised self-sufficiency and pig clubs were set up to encourage pig keeping. Despite this brief revival, the number of households keeping their own pigs never again matched the levels seen in the previous century. Indeed, by the middle of the twentieth century, as more and more factory-produced pork became available, keeping pigs for personal consumption had largely become a thing of the past.

THE RITUAL OF KILLING

The killing of a pig in a eighteenth- and nineteenth-century village was often a huge social occasion involving the whole neighbourhood, with men, women and children all playing their part in the process. Certain rituals often had to be carried out and these varied from region to region. Superstitions had to be observed, too – in some regions in Ireland, for example, pigs could never be killed unless there was an 'R' in the month, while in other places it was believed that a pig killed under a full moon would give more meat. Large farms would often kill several pigs on one day and the families associated with the farm would have access to meat for many, many months.

Opposite page: **Pigs have played an important role since the days of early man.**

The slaughtering of the animal would be done by the men, while the women would be responsible for the processing of the meat, with help from the children. No part of the pig was wasted – everything was used, from the ears, cheeks and snout down to the trotters. Delicacies such as pig's fry (pieces of innards rolled in seasoned flour) were popular and consumed quickly. Ears were turned into pies. Meat from the head was potted or pickled. The fat would be turned into lard. Arguably the best product of all, though, was the bacon, which would be salted in a process that would sometimes take up to six weeks. Along with the hams, it would be hung from the cottage rafters to be cut from when required. Bacon cured in this way would keep for many months and was therefore a favourite food staple on board ships.

In other countries too, the killing of a pig was almost always accompanied by celebrations. In America prior to the Civil War, pigs were considered a food staple in the south. They were cheap to maintain and could live on the nuts, berries and roots as well as tubers, worms and grubs in the surrounding forests. Whole families were often invited to share in the eating after a killing, and it was these gatherings that give birth to the traditional southern barbecue.

CHANGING MARKETS

Important improvements to the selection and breeding of pigs in Britain continued over the centuries. During the eighteenth and nineteenth centuries many of the breeds changed almost beyond recognition, with the introduction of prick-eared pigs of Chinese and Siamese bloodlines. Their influence on the existing breeds

Prick-eared pigs of Asian origin were used to improve breeds such as the Berkshire.

The Lincolnshire Curly Coat unfortunately became extinct in the early 1970s.

resulted in many of the traditional breeds that are available today. One traditional breed that was not influenced by these bloodlines, however, was the Tamworth, which remains today the closest relative of the wild boar.

Changing fashion and market requirements have had a major influence on the ways in which traditional breeds have fared over the years. Up to the 1930s, breeds had been developed to suit a particular market and had a major role in commercial production. Specialist pork and bacon pigs such as the Berkshire and the Middle White were in much demand, as were the fattier lard pigs such as the Mangalitza. As a result, these were the breeds that thrived.

In the 1930s, the Middle White and Berkshire started to decline as the Large White and the Essex and Wessex breeds (now known as the British Saddleback after an amalgamation in 1967) took their place. Fashion and market requirements dictated change again in 1952, when the popularity of the Large White overtook that of the Essex and Wessex, with the Large White becoming one of the most influential breeds in commercial pork production. This is the situation that prevails to this day.

In 1955, in order to satisfy market requirements, a decision was made to focus on only three breeds of pigs: the Large White, the Landrace and the Welsh. This had disastrous consequences on the traditional breeds, with the result that by 1973 most of them had declined to such low levels that they were in danger of being lost for ever. Some breeds had already been lost and it was only through the determination of a handful of breeders, and the support of the Rare Breeds Survival Trust, that many of the breeds were saved from extinction.

THE FUTURE

Although the future of Britain's traditional breeds currently seems safe, there is no room for complacency. The tide can easily turn, and once more those breeds could be fighting for survival. With pig keepers no longer allowed to feed pigs on waste products, due to the risk of disease, the cost of keeping them has dramatically increased over the years.

Despite this, the future does look bright. Britain's attitude to food and its provenance seems to be changing. A significant number of people now prefer to buy food from locally bred animals that have led a more natural life, than from those that have lived in an intensive unit. Consumers are beginning to appreciate that fat really does mean more taste and are turning their backs on the more bland meat that is offered to us by supermarkets.

Farm shops are springing up everywhere, pork is being sold straight from the farm through the internet and farmers' markets are flourishing. Even some butchers are now bowing to customer demand and selling the meat from traditional breeds in their shops. The British Pig Association has seen a steady growth in new members, pig equipment companies have never had it so good and breeders have waiting lists for their litters. What is going on?

Breeds such as the Mangalitza were once renowned for their lard but are now used for specialist meats.

Celebrity chefs in part have helped promote this surge of interest in self-sufficiency and the growth in sales of traditional pork. Celebrities who own herds of traditional breeds, such as the actress Elizabeth Hurley and the chef Anthony Worrell Thompson, have made pig keeping fashionable. The most sought-after breeds are inevitably the more 'attractive' ones, such as the Oxford Sandy and Black, Gloucester Old Spot and the British Saddleback. Breeds such as the British Lop and the Welsh are not as popular, due in part to their plain colour and their similarity in appearance to intensively bred pigs.

During the Second World War, the nation's population was encouraged to tighten its belt and practise self-sufficiency. Once again, although not for the same reasons, people are increasingly looking to produce themselves the food they eat. Some no longer trust the supermarkets to deliver on taste and quality and, as more and more people are realizing that it is possible to keep a couple of pigs for the freezer easily and reasonably cheaply, so the demand is growing.

A recent growth in the specialist market of cured meats has seen a significant upturn in the numbers of lard breeds such as the Mangalitza and others. A breed that was once so popular its meat was sold on the Vienna stock exchange, it had declined to fewer than 100 in just a few years. Specialist meats such as Parma ham and salamis are fetching a premium and breeds such as the Mangalitza and the European Iberian pig are crucial to this market.

To ensure the future of the traditional breeds, people must eat them, either raising them themselves, or buying from keepers who do so. This is the only way to make sure that these wonderful creatures survive.

PORK AND RELIGION

The pig has been considered an unclean animal by some religions and this is still the case today. Early Christians shunned pork up until AD50, when laws banning the eating of the meat were relaxed. Muhammad also banned the eating of pork and the pig population of the Middle East and Western Asia declined rapidly because of this.

CHAPTER 2

Choosing the Right Pig

WHICH BREED?

Choosing your first pigs is a task not to be undertaken lightly. A pig can grow into a fairly large beast and, therefore, when becoming a pig owner for the first time, you need to be sure not only that you have picked a breed that you like, but also that you will be able to meet their welfare needs, and that you are able to handle them comfortably on a day-to-day basis.

The first question to ask yourself is why you want to keep pigs. Do you want them for the freezer, for instance, or as pets? As a tool? For your land or for breeding? The answers to these vital questions will point you towards the most suitable breed for your requirements.

There are many factors to take into account, especially if you are buying a pig for a specific reason. The appearance of a breed should not be the main consideration when you are looking at the different types, although of course you might consider it important to like the look of it. Lack of knowledge of a particular breed, or choosing the wrong pig for your situation and requirements, could lead not only to disappointments, but also to all sorts of problems, including possible handler injuries.

To avoid making what could be an expensive and disappointing mistake, you need to be absolutely clear in your mind what you are actually buying the pig for, to enable you to pick a suitable breed. If it is for meat, you need to have a good idea as to what you intend to do with the carcass. For example, some pigs are better for bacon than for pork, while others are great for specialized meats such as Parma ham. If you are new to pig keeping and you would like a pig that gives you a bit of everything – joints as well as bacon and sausages – it is usually advisable to start off with a good all-round pig such as the Large Black or the British Lop. They are easy to look after, and they also give delicious pork as well as bacon. When you gain more experience and knowledge, you may want to start experimenting with keeping other, more demanding breeds, or even trying your hand at crossing breeds.

A knowledge of which breeds are best for which cuts can only come through research and also tastings of the different types of breeds. Some breeds are leaner than others, and produce a 'gamier' meat, while breeds such as the Gloucester Old Spot are more fatty and are better for joints rather than bacon. Today, it is possible to buy meat online from every single traditional breed, as well as wild boar and even the wild boar/Tamworth cross, the Iron Age pig. Testing the different tastes and textures from the breeds is definitely worth doing if you are looking at keeping pigs to fill your freezer. Farmers' markets

Choose a docile breed if you have a young family.

and farm shops are a good place to look for traditional pork and it is even worth enquiring at your local butcher's. More and more butchers are realizing that the market for these types of pigs is on the increase and therefore it is not unusual to find pork from traditional breeds sitting alongside the more commercial meat. However, do not forget to check with your butcher which breed you are trying, otherwise you will be none the wiser when tasting it!

Traditional Breeds

Traditional breeds as a rule are very hardy, usually withstanding all types of climate. However, some breeds are hardier than others. Most, if not all, are affected by the cold in one way or another and, if you are planning to raise pigs for the freezer, thought should be given to this if you live in a harsher climate. Hairy pigs such as the Tamworth, Duroc or the Mangalitza are exceptional hardy and do well whatever the conditions. White breeds such as the Landrace and the British Lop are less hardy, due to their relatively thin skin and white coat. Keeping their condition could be a problem in a tougher climate.

In the UK, and especially in the north, pigs are likely to have to endure very cold or prolonged wet weather. This can have an effect on the weight gain of your pigs, no matter how hardy they are, and they could even suffer weight loss as they use up their fat reserves to keep warm. This could prove expensive, if you are trying to fatten them up for the freezer. Your food

Both parents have to be registered with the BPA for the offspring to be eligible for registration.

costs will increase as you pump extra food into them to try and keep the weight on, or their weight gain may be slower, which means keeping them longer until they reach the required weight.

Some breeders, no matter where they live, swear by insulated arks in the winter to keep the ark temperature constant. In this way, they avoid exposing their pigs to fluctuating temperatures, which, again, could have an effect on weight gain. Certainly, anything that helps keep the pigs warm is worth considering in cold weather, regardless of the reason why you are keeping the pigs. All breeds of pig need dry shelter facing away from the prevailing wind.

Over-heating can also be a problem for pigs. Saddlebacks and Large Blacks are known for their tolerance of hot weather (as well as being capable of withstanding cold temperatures), and these breeds are often exported to warmer countries.

Pedigree or Cross-Breed?

As with any animal, buying a pure-bred pedigree more or less guarantees that you are getting what you pay for – a pure-bred animal whose line you can trace a few generations back. You know almost 100 per cent how big the animal will grow, what it will look like and, in the case of a pig, the type of meat it will produce. The same cannot be said of a cross-breed.

A pedigree pig is a pure-bred pig that has been registered with the British Pig Association. To register a litter, both parents have to be pure-bred and registered with the British Pig Association. It is not possible to register a litter if one or both of the parents are unregistered. Even when

Opposite page: **Make sure you choose the correct breed for your requirements.**

the unregistered parent is a pure-bred from registered stock, unless it is registered as well, it is just another pig. Many novice pig keepers do not understand the difference between a pure-bred and a pedigree. 'Pure-bred' does not signify 'pedigree' and therefore you have only the breeder's word that the pig you are buying is a pure breed.

Cross-breeds certainly have their place. Research and investment by large commercial farms and companies, especially in the USA, have gone into cross-breeding programmes to ensure that the progeny of two different breeds conform to prevailing market requirements. Even for smallholders, cross-breeds can be useful if they are planning to sell at farmers' markets and want to present a leaner meat to their customers. For the novice, however, it is not advisable to buy anything other than pedigree pure-breeds. Even the very experienced can only guess at how the weaner from two different breeds will turn out. If you choose an unknown cross-bred, there is no guarantee that you will get the quality of meat you require. Depending on what it has been crossed with, its temperament could also be questionable, which could prove disastrous for a novice pig keeper. Buying a cross-bred is initially cheaper but it will cost the same to keep so it is worth spending the extra £20 or £30 at the beginning for a registered pedigree pig. By buying a registered breed most of the guesswork as to how it will turn out has been taken away, plus you have the support of the breed society, as well as knowing you are in a small way helping to keep these vulnerable breeds going.

If you are planning to keep a pig only as a pet, cross-breeds are definitely not suitable, as it is vital that you are sure of what you are taking on. Pet pigs tend to be kept by families in a relatively small area, so they need to be quite small, have a predictable temperament and be easy to manage.

TEMPERAMENT

The most important factor to consider when purchasing pigs for the first time is temperament. Much has been written about the personality of the different breeds and the ways in which some, especially the prick-eared, are more boisterous than the lop-eared. Overall this tends to be true, with lop-eared pigs being a lot quieter and easier to handle than their prick-eared relatives, probably because the ears cover the eyes and their view is restricted. However, much does depend on how they were bred and raised. There are many breeders who seem to be able to raise prick-eared pigs such as Tamworths that end up being the quietest of animals. If you are a novice, and a prick-eared pig ticks all the right boxes for you, do not be put off by the fact that it is known for being a bit of handful. You just need to find the right breeder.

If you do decide to go for a prick-eared breed such as a Tamworth, you need to proceed carefully. Never buy any pig unseen. Visit as many breeders as you can, and try to go on recommendations from other pig owners. If possible, spend all day helping the breeder with their pigs; as long as you take care not to get in the way, time-strapped breeders may appreciate any help with the mundane chores. Ask yourself a number of questions. Do you feel safe handling the animals? Are the weaners friendly or do they come across as nervy? Have they been consistently handled? Does the breeder seem happy to handle the boars? Do you feel comfortable with the size of the pigs? Most importantly,

Opposite page: **Tamworths can make good novice pigs, but you need to proceed with caution.**

is the breeder willing to be at the end of the telephone if you have a problem or need advice? If the answer to all of these questions is 'yes', and you have sufficient land, there is no reason why your first pig should not be a prick-eared one.

MALE OR FEMALE?

Many people refuse to buy male pigs for fear that they might have problems with 'boar taint', a term that refers to a very strong gamey smell that can be present in boars. However, this is rare in traditional breeds that have been living free range, and is more usually associated with intensively kept pigs.

PIG COURSES

A few years ago, if you wanted to learn how to keep pigs you would attend a college course specializing in animal husbandry, which would cover not only pigs, but also every other farm animal. Now that pig keeping is becoming more fashionable, specific pig courses are being offered in all sorts of venues. Breeders use courses as a way of bringing in extra revenue for what can be quite an expensive business. All-day courses – good and bad – usually cost around £100, so it is vital to choose carefully. Avoid courses that cater for large groups of students. Smaller numbers do not necessarily mean that a course is good, but in a larger group you may have to wait a long time before you actually get to have a go at handling the pigs or practising tattooing or slap-marking. It might also mean that the person running the course cares more for how much money it is bringing in, rather than ensuring that students go away with a good background

knowledge and the confidence to go out and buy and look after their own pigs. Ideally, you should go on recommendation, but in the absence of that, do not be afraid of ringing a breeder up and finding out as much as possible about the content of the course and what percentage is taken up with actually handling the pigs.

Anyone keeping pigs for the first time should try to spend a day with the animals, either as work experience or paying for the pleasure. Pigs are easy to look after, but there are a number of pitfalls that could be avoided with advance knowledge. Attending a course will give you an idea as to whether you are ready for pigs.

AGRICULTURAL SHOWS

If your knowledge of the different pig breeds amounts to nothing more than the fact that there are 'pink' pigs and coloured pigs, a good place to start is by attending the pig classes at an agricultural show, usually held during the summer. Not only will you get to see every traditional pig in one place, you will also be able to chat to the breeders in the pig lines and formulate a better idea of which breed would suit your requirements. Breeders love talking about their pigs, especially if they think there will be a sale in it if for them, so take advantage of this by taking the time to discuss your plans with as many different breeders as possible.

Seeing the crème de la crème of pigs will also give you an idea as to what a good pig should look like, thereby hopefully making it easier to choose when looking through a group of weaners. It is also a fun challenge to try and pick the winner; if you are wrong, try and speak to the judge afterwards and find out why they picked the winning pig. Developing an eye for a good pig takes time. Some people have the gift instinctively, but the majority have to learn the skill over a number of years, more often than not making mistakes along the way.

URBAN VS. RURAL

Right up to the end of the Second World War in Britain, pigs were often kept by town dwellers in a back yard, providing a good and regular source of meat for their families. Today, though, things have changed. Local councils do not want to encourage suburban families keeping what is essentially a farm animal in such an environment. Certain prejudices against the pig have probably helped bring this about, as well as the change in attitude towards food and where it comes from. People no longer have to keep animals to

feed themselves; they simply hop in their car and visit the supermarket. A detachment has grown over the years between what they eat and its source. Fresh meat has also become much more accessible to the ordinary person and it is certainly much cheaper to buy than it was many years ago.

Slowly, the situation is changing again, with an upsurge in people looking to produce their own food. This is thanks in part to a few well-known journalists and chefs investigating what really goes on behind the mass production of food, revealing that the food on your plate is not always what is seems. Another factor is taste – cheaper supermarket bacon, for example, is almost always of a lower quality than home-cured bacon. Even the most expensive supermarket bacon sometimes oozes with the globules of brine with which it has been injected. Similarly, the difference, in terms

Summer is the best time to keep pigs if you live in an urban area

of colour, texture and fat, between a mass-produced joint and pork from your own pig is quite startling.

It is certainly possible nowadays to keep not only chickens in your back garden, but also pigs. As long as you choose the right breed for your location, there is no reason why you should not become an urban pig farmer, with your pigs enjoying exactly the same quality of life as a rural pig.

Some breeds are better suited than others to living in a smaller space. It could be argued that most urban farmers keep their pigs only a few months before sending them off to the abattoir, and that the size of pig is therefore irrelevant – all breeds are of a more or less similar size when they go at five or six months. However, should you want to keep your pig longer for bacon, you should choose a smaller breed, which will end up no bigger than medium-sized and will remain manageable. Medium-sized breeds such as the Berkshire and the Middle White have proved popular in the past as 'garden' pigs, while the Kune Kune, an even smaller breed, is also ideal for this use. Due to their size, however, the length of time you have to keep these breeds before they are ready for killing is usually around 12–18 months. This is probably longer than you would keep one of the larger breeds and, even after all that time, the joints will still be much smaller than from other breeds. As a result, many people keep them just for pets or for breeding. There is another problem with these breeds: because they are so friendly, it can make it much more difficult when it comes to sending them to the abattoir and eating their meat!

Breeds such as the Tamworth are not suitable for keeping in the garden due to their temperament and their need for free-ranging, and of course their ability to escape. Who could forget the entertaining story of the 'Tamworth Two', who avoided the slaughterhouse by going on the run in the Gloucestershire countryside?

When considering keeping pigs in an urban back garden, it is very important to look at your plans from the perspective of your neighbours. You must communicate with them to iron out any potential problems before the pigs arrive. You may also need to spend a little more time preparing for your pigs than you would if you lived in a more rural setting.

BREEDS

There follows here a brief description of each of the fifteen traditional and modern breeds that are found in the UK as well as a description of the wild boar and the cross-bred Iron-Age pig. Not all are suitable for keeping simply as a couple of pigs for the personal freezer. Some such as the wild boar need specialist care, a Dangerous Wild Animal licence and lots of space in which to live as natural a life as possible.

As this is primarily a book on pigs for the freezer, descriptions of suitable pigs for pets have not been included. In some parts of the UK, some breeds may be harder to locate than others.

Traditional Breeds

Tamworth
The prick-eared Tamworth is one of the UK's oldest breeds, originating in the town of Tamworth in the Midlands. Unlike other breeds, the Tamworth was not crossed with Chinese stock to improve it and therefore remains a close representation of Britain's first indigenous pigs. It is a good-tempered pig but it can be mischievous and challenging on occasions, especially for novices.

Tamworth.

The Tamworth's striking red coat will brighten up many a dull day, but its abundant hair can pose a problem at abattoirs. You will need to check with an abattoir before you take a Tamworth in, as some refuse to de-hair them, preferring instead to skin them. This of course will result in a loss of crackling.

Many years ago the Tamworth was kept by both farmers and cottagers, who used the pig for bacon that they cured themselves at home. Unfortunately, after the Second World War, numbers of Tamworths declined to such an extent that during the 1970s there were only seventeen surviving boars.

Tamworths are ideally suited to wooded areas although they are equally at home on pasture. They tend not to be suitable for gardens and indoor intensive farms. They have fantastic rooting abilities that can turn over a patch of land within hours, so they are not suitable for front lawns!

The slow-growing Tamworth is primarily an excellent bacon pig with a lean body and large hams. The texture of the meat is fine, sweet-tasting and full-flavoured. It is pale in colour and, when the skin is left on, produces superb crackling.

British Lop

Known originally as the Devon or Cornish Lop in the Tavistock area of Devon where it was first recognized, this breed was extremely popular with farmers in the surrounding areas, who very wisely kept this excellent pork and bacon pig to themselves. Over time, however, the Lop did spread over the West Country but it never really found the favour it had enjoyed in its native county. First registered as the 'National Long White Lop-Eared', its name was shortened to the 'British Lop' and it was taken under the wing of the Rare Breed Survival Trust in 1973, as numbers were dangerously low.

Even today, the British Lop is still one of the rarest of all the traditional breeds; this could be attributed in part to its indistinctive looks. Fans of traditional breeds usually want pigs that look traditional, not ones that could pass for an ordinary commercial pig.

Like many of the traditional breeds, an outdoor free-range environment suits this pig. Although it is hardy, care must be taken in the summer as its white fine coat makes it susceptible to sunburn; shelter and a wallow are a must.

Pig keepers who do buy a British Lop will be rewarded with an extremely friendly, docile pig that is easy to handle in all ways. They make good mothers, usually farrowing large litters of fifteen to sixteen piglets quite easily, so they are ideal for the novice breeder.

The Lop's long, lean body produces quality pork and bacon and usually finishes with a well-muscled carcass.

Large Black

The Large Black has the distinction of being the only all-black pig in Britain and is believed to have originated from the Old English Hog dating back to the sixteenth and seventeenth centuries. In the late 1800s, the Large Black was found mainly in East Anglia and Devon and Cornwall. Although the pigs found in both areas were black, there was a difference in type between the two areas, with the pigs of East Anglia being smaller and fatter than their cousins in the south-west.

Despite being an extremely large pig,

British Lop.

Large Black.

the lop-eared Large Black is ideal for beginners. One of the hardiest of all traditional breeds, its black skin makes it perfect for hot climates and, by 1935, the breed had been exported to over thirty different countries.

In 1889 the Large Black Society was founded and the breed's popularity continued to grow until the 1960s, when, in common with many of the other traditional breeds, it saw a considerable decline in numbers. In 1973, the breed was placed on the critical list of the Rare Breed Society Trust. Nowadays, however, its popularity is on the increase again as more and more smallholders are recognizing the benefits of keeping it.

Often known as the 'Elephant' pig because of the enormous long ears covering its face, this is definitely a good all-round pig to start with for smallholders. It is especially suitable for families as its placid temperament makes it ideal for children to handle. It is also a low-maintenance pig that efficiently converts grass to protein.

The Large Black produces succulent pork with a delicate taste that makes the meat enjoyable to eat either hot or cold. Unlike other breeds it does not tend to suffer from too much back fat and, despite the pig itself being black, the meat is reasonably pale.

Berkshire.

Berkshire

Otherwise known as the 'Ladies' Pig' because of its delicate and pretty features, the Berkshire is renowned throughout the world for its succulent pork, especially in Japan where it is marketed as 'Black Pork' and sold at a premium price. The earliest record of the Berkshire was made by Cromwell's troops when they were stationed at Reading; they were particularly appreciative of its bacon and ham qualities.

Today's Berkshire is smaller than the larger and coarser pig of Cromwell's times, having been heavily influenced by the introduction of Chinese and Siamese blood. This cross-breeding resulted in the smaller black pig, with prick ears and white socks and a white tip to its tail, that is familiar today.

At one point in the nineteenth century the Berkshire was so popular that it was even owned by members of royalty. However, like other traditional breeds, its popularity began to wane after the Second World War, as breeding companies focused on the white breeds.

Nowadays, the popularity of the Berkshire is on the rise again, as more and more smallholders appreciate its compact size, its succulent meat and its docile temperament. Although prick-eared, it tends not to have the mischievous qualities of those types and is an ideal starter pig for the urbanite.

Although the breed is black, the meat dresses out white and produces superb pork joints with a mouth-watering taste and excellent crackling.

British Saddleback

The British Saddleback breed came about after the herd books of two similar types of pigs – the Wessex from the New Forest and the Essex – were amalgamated in 1967 and a new herd book was started. Both pigs were black with a white band passing over the back and front legs, but the Essex also had a white tip to its tail. The Essex was known as the 'Gents' Pig' because it was considered fancier than the Wessex, which was known as the 'Farmers' Pig'.

The Saddleback, like many of the traditional breeds, prefers to live outdoors and, as it tends to graze rather than root, it is ideal for keeping on pastureland. It is one of the hardier pigs; the black pigmentation in its skin offers good protection against the sun, although it is always a good idea to keep an eye on the saddle in hot weather, as it is not unknown for the pink part of its skin to suffer sunburn.

The lop-eared Saddleback is ideal for families as, like the Large Black, it is a docile pig that is easy-going and easy to handle.

British Saddleback meat is full-flavoured and succulent, with excellent crackling. It does carry more fat than some of the other breeds, but the juices from this only add to the succulence and flavour of the meat. Sometimes there is prejudice against the Saddleback as many people think that, because it is black, it will produce black crackling or bacon rind. This is not the case and, once the bristles have been removed, the Saddleback has similar skin to any other pig.

British Saddleback.

Gloucester Old Spot.

Gloucester Old Spot

The Gloucester Old Spot is one of the best starter pigs for novices and families with young children. It is very gentle, although it can on occasion be incredibly stubborn. The Old Spot is safe around children but it can be really difficult to work with if you are asking it to do something it does not want to do, such as moving between pens or being loaded into a trailer. Nothing will encourage it to move if it does not want to. It is precisely this stubborn gentle character that has helped to make it one of the best-loved pigs of all times.

The Gloucester Old Spot has been around for over two centuries but was officially recognized only in 1913. It was also known also as the 'orchard pig', because it was kept on the windfalls in the orchards of Gloucestershire, and legend has it that its spots were caused by apples falling from the trees and bruising the skin.

Nowadays, the Old Spot is one of the most prolific of all the traditional breeds, with many novice pig keepers choosing to start off with it.

The Gloucester Old Spot is better known for its capacity to produce large, succulent-tasting joints rather than bacon. Although it is perfectly possible to take bacon off a Gloucester, its tendency to form back fat quite quickly can prove problematic when bringing it up to bacon weight. It also makes for very good sausages.

The Gloucester is definitely a pig that should be kept outside, preferably on

Oxford Sandy and Black.

grass rather than woodland. As it does not tend to be an escape artist, unlike some of the other breeds, it can be kept behind a couple of strands of electric wire a few inches off the ground, once it has become accustomed to the restriction. This is particularly helpful if you are wanting to strip-graze your land.

Oxford Sandy and Black

This is one of the most attractive of all the traditional breeds, with colours ranging from shades of sandy to a rich copper marked with black blotches. Once known as the 'Plum Pudding Pig' and the 'Oxford Forest Pig', the Oxford Sandy has been on the brink of extinction more than once. Nowadays however, its attractive appear-

ance and its docile temperament make it a firm favourite with smallholders, and numbers are growing. A hardy animal, it adapts well to all climates, especially the cold as its abundance of hair helps to keep it warm.

It is a pig that should be allowed as much freedom as possible in either woodland or pasture environment, as it is a natural grazer and loves to forage.

It is a multi-purpose, reasonably lean pig that tends to be lighter-boned than some of the other breeds, and has a good ratio of meat to bone when slaughtered. Good for bacon and having superb hams, it does not tend to suffer from excess fat, unlike some of the other breeds.

Middle White

An ideal pig for the garden, the Middle White is a docile, medium-sized pig that is perfect for beginners and those who live in an urban area. With its 'dished' face and 'squashed' nose, it has often been compared in appearance to a bat, and has even been considered by some to be ugly. However, for smallholders who do not wish to see their land rooted up, it is an ideal breed as it does not have the tendency to root as much as other longer-snouted breeds.

The breed was first recognized in 1852 and soon found favour with London butchers for its succulent pork and its early maturing, which sometimes led to it affectionately being known as the 'London Porker'.

The breed kept going from strength to strength until after the Second World War. when numbers fell dramatically, as the demand for bacon pigs increased and pork pigs were sidelined. Today, the numbers are once again on the increase. Well-known chef Anthony Worrell Thompson is patron of the Middle White Breeders' Club and the breed has become much favoured by London restaurants for its wonderful suckling pigs.

As with the Berkshire breed, quality breeding stock is regularly exported worldwide, in particular to Japan, where it is known as the 'Middle Yorks'.

The Middle White is an easy pig to keep and matures early.

Mangalitza

A relative newcomer to the UK, the Mangalitza is slowly growing in numbers as more and more smallholders are realizing the benefits of owning the breed. It was

Middle White.

Mangalitza.

first imported into the country in 2006, and there are now seven female lines and three boars' lines established.

Popular in countries such as Austria, Germany and Hungary, where it is found in large numbers foraging in woodland, the Mangalitza is perfect for specialist meats such as salamis. It is also known as a lard pig and can produce up to 70 litres of lard.

It is a primitive breed, docile but at the same time quite lively. The breed comes in three colours, which vary in size. The Red is the largest, the Swallow-Bellied is the medium-sized and the Blonde is the smallest. All colours have a woolly, curly coat and from a distance some of the pigs could be mistaken for sheep.

An incredibly hardy pig, the Mangalitza has a coat that is shorter and straighter in the summer when it moults. It keeps the pig warm in winter and prevents it from getting sunburn in the summer.

The Mangalitza is very slow-growing and can take up to two years to reach 100kg, however the meat is of fantastic quality and ideal for air dried and cured meat.

Mangalitzas are suitable only for outdoor management.

Modern Breeds

Landrace

The British Landrace is one of the modern breeds suitable for both indoor systems and outdoor. Consequently, this pig has not really caught on as far as smallholders are concerned, even though it is of a docile nature and very easy to handle.

Its name derives from the German term for 'national breed' and today most European countries as well as Canada

Landrace.

and the United States have their own 'Landrace'. In 1949 Britain imported four boars and eight gilts from Sweden and it was at this time that the Breed Society was first established. The herd book was created in 1950 from the first piglets from that importation.

The Landrace is a lean pig, long in body with full hams. It is one of the most important pigs in the commercial world, and without a doubt anyone who has ever eaten supermarket pork will at one time or another have tasted the Landrace or a Landrace cross.

As it has been specially bred to reach the required weight more quickly than traditional breeds, and spends most of its life indoors, it does not have the depth of taste or the succulence that other more traditional, slower-growing breeds have. Its leanness of carcass means that it is very good as a bacon pig as well as being good for joints.

The Landrace has an ability to improve other breeds and can be of use to smallholders who are interested crossing it with a slower-growing breed to produce a leaner progeny.

Duroc

The Duroc originated in the USA from the early 'Red Hogs' bred in New York and New Jersey. Today's Duroc is a cross between Red Durocs from New York and Jersey Red Hogs from New Jersey. It was first introduced in Britain in the 1970s. The Duroc is not usually at the top of the list of possible breeds for smallholders, perhaps because it is not as attractive as some of the other breeds, and also because it has always been associated with the commercial market.

The Duroc is an extremely hardy, low-maintenance pig with a reasonable nature. It has attractive thick auburn winter hair, which moults dramatically in the summer,

Duroc.

leaving the pig almost bald. It has a reasonably docile temperament, which makes it ideal for novices who want something a bit more challenging than a lop-eared pig.

The Duroc is known for its tender and tasty meat and in the USA it is the second most frequently recorded breed of swine, where it is used not only for light pork but also for heavy hog production.

If you are looking for a pig for the freezer, this is a good breed to add to your list of possibles.

Welsh

Although slowly growing in popularity outside of its native Wales, the Welsh breed is still one of the rarest of all the breeds.

In common with the British Lop, it has a plainness of appearance and colour that seems to discourage traditional breed enthusiasts from keeping it, even though its docile temperament and its wonderful meat make it an excellent pig for families and beginners.

Welsh pigs were first referred to in the 1870s, when, along with Shropshire pigs, they were sent to Cheshire for fattening on milk by-products. It was not until 1922, however, that the Welsh Pig Society as it is known today was formed, following the amalgamation of two Welsh breed societies.

In recent times, the Welsh Assembly has involved itself in the future of the breed,

Welsh.

promising to make funds available to help develop the breed.

The Welsh prospered right up until the 1980s, when the number of registrations declined rapidly. Certainly, outside of Wales, they are harder to come by and, if you live in another part of the UK, you may have to travel some distance to find a breeder.

It is a reasonably lean pig that is easy to handle and adapts to any situation, both indoors and out. It is ideal for both pork and bacon, has a fast liveweight gain and a good killing-out percentage. It is also a good breed to cross with other more traditional breeds.

Although it is known for its hardiness, its white skin can make it susceptible to sunburn, and shelter and a wallow are a must in summer.

They make excellent mothers and have large litters.

Pietrain

The Pietrain takes its name from the village of Pietrain in Belgium where it has been raised since 1920. Officially established in 1956, it has become one of the most important commercial breeds in European pig-producing countries and is used widely to improve other breeds. First exported to the UK in 1964 by the Pig Industry Development Authority, it has never really taken off as a smallholder pig.

The Pietrain is a medium-sized pig with huge bulging muscles on its shoulders and hams. Although on the whole it is quite easy to handle, it can at times display aggressive tendencies, especially when it has a litter, so it is not really suitable for total novices.

It produces fat-free meat, which means in real terms that no more than a quarter of an inch of fat should be found on its back.

It can be kept inside or out, but is usually found in indoor intensive units. If kept outside, it will need to be observed carefully in the summer for any signs of sunburn.

Hampshire

Although similar to the British Saddleback, the Hampshire has never reached the

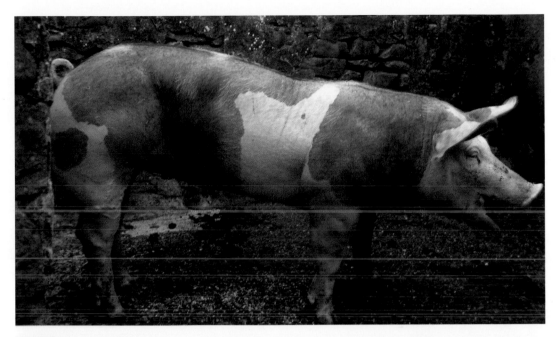

Pietrain.

Hampshire.

Large White.

same degree of popularity with smallholders as that breed. Even though it shares some attributes, such as a docile temperament and an ability to do well in any environment, it is a breed that is more usually associated with commercial enterprises than with smallholding.

Developed in the USA, the Hampshire is considered by many in the commercial world to be the best terminal sire breed for all purposes. The majority of carcass competitions in North America are often won by Hampshire or Hampshire crosses.

It is a large, heavily muscled animal, with an extremely large snout and the same colouring and markings as the Saddleback. Unlike the Saddleback, however, it has minimal amounts of back fat and large loin eyes.

There are only a few specialized smaller breeders in the UK and therefore the breed can be difficult to locate.

Large White

In common with other modern breeds, the Large White is usually associated with commercial units. With its origins in the Yorkshire pig, now extinct in the UK, it was one of the original founder breeds of the National Pig Breeders' Association (now known as the British Pig Association). The Large White was exported all over the world to meet the demand for quality British-bred breeding stock. Consequently, this breed can be found in many cross-bred breeding programmes and has become an important breed in most of the pig-producing countries in the world.

It can be kept indoors or out, but care has to be taken in the summer when its white skin is susceptible to sunburn.

The breed is used extensively in cross-breeding programmes as it has the ability to improve other breeds. Like many of the traditional breeds, it is late in maturing and is thought on the whole to have poor ham development.

It is a large breed, with prick ears, long legs and a dished face.

Large Whites are good mothers, with an abundance of milk and farrowing large litters of between twelve and fourteen.

Other Breeds

Iron Age

In the 1970s, a research project was undertaken to reconstruct a pig that would have lived in Britain in the Iron Age. The Tamworth and the wild boar were chosen as the two breeds most likely to produce progeny similar to that of an ancient pig. The resulting breed is definitely not a pig for beginners and even those with some experience under their belt should proceed with caution if they do decide to take on an Iron Age.

The Iron Age has the characteristics of both parents: the aggressiveness of the wild boar and the lively tendencies of the Tamworth. Those who do manage to cope with keeping the breed will be rewarded with lean, gamey meat and, if the skin is left on, superb crackling.

The Iron Age is a low-maintenance pig, which is happiest living in woodland, where it can do what it does best: rooting and foraging. It prefers to nest naturally, finding

Iron Age.

a hollow of a tree rather than sleeping in a man-made shelter, which it would probably destroy anyway. Fencing must be the best you can afford, erected professionally and checked regularly.

The colour of this pig can be either red like the Tamworth or grey brown like the wild boar. Some can be nearly black.

It has bristlier hair (which, like the Tamworth, could prove a problem when at the abattoir), prick ears and a long snout. Loading it into a trailer can often prove problematic as well; preparation and lots of patience are definitely the key to successful loading.

It makes a superb mother, raising piglets that are born striped like the young of the wild boar and the Mangalitza.

Wild Boar

Hunted to extinction in Scotland in the seventeenth or eighteenth century, and earlier than that in England, the wild boar is starting to make a significant comeback. The great storms in Britain in 1989 not only destroyed over a million trees but also enabled large numbers of wild boar to escape from their enclosures into the countryside. No one really knows how many are living wild but there is no doubt that, as they breed, wild boar will once again become a main feature of the UK, as in other European countries such as France and Germany.

Wild boar are incredibly hardy, preferring to live in dense woodland rather than out in the open. Males are solitary but females are very social and live in groups known as 'soundings'. They hunt usually at night, feeding on mice, roots, worms and berries.

Although shy, they can be very aggressive, especially if they are guarding their young. Farmers who wish to keep pure

Wild Boar.

All traditional breeds are hardy.

wild boar have to apply for a licence and fulfil certain conditions before this will be granted.

Wild boar has been on the menu of the nobility for thousands of years, with much importance placed on its head at festive feasts, as Mrs Beeton recorded in her *Book of Household Management* in 1861:

> The Boar's head, in ancient times, formed the most important dish on the table, and was invariably the first placed on the board at festive feasts, being preceded by a body of servitors, a flourish of trumpets, and other marks of distinction and reverence, and carried into the hall by the individual of next rank to the lord of the feast.

Wild boar grow very slowly, usually taking between twelve and fourteen months to mature up to the size of a porker, which can be costly to the farmer. The meat is dark, has a strong gamey flavour and is low in fat. It is usually sold at specialist outlets.

The sow will produce between four and nine stripy young, known as boarlets.

Whichever breed you choose to fill your freezer, you will have the satisfaction of knowing, when you sit down to your first home-produced joint, exactly how that pig has been raised and what it has been fed on.

CHAPTER 3

Getting Started

EQUIPMENT PRIORITIES

For the novice, the amount of pig equipment and arks on the market can be mind-boggling. There are always new companies marketing pig equipment, and working out what you really need and what you can do without for your weaners, can be confusing to the less experienced.

When looking at keeping a couple of pigs for the freezer, you do not require an endless supply of money, masses of specialized equipment or loads of space in which to keep them. Two pigs can be kept on very little land, without compromising their welfare, and the amount of equipment needed is surprisingly small.

If your budget is tight, most equipment – such as ready-made arks – that is available from specialist companies can be substituted with something else. The same is true of feed and water utensils. However, it is worth bearing in mind that, if you do substitute equipment with something that is not really intended for use with pigs, it may not last the course and could end up

Well-constructed stock fencing will last for years.

costing you more in the long run. Go on recommendation, many arks appear solid and well made, but often when they are used by destructive pigs, they don't last five minutes.

The one thing that you should never skimp on is fencing, and unfortunately this will usually represent your greatest outlay when preparing for your pigs, unless you are lucky enough to be in the fencing trade. Whether you are keeping pigs in an urban or rural setting, fencing is the most important thing to get right. Unless the fencing is sturdy, well built and fit for the purpose of keeping your pigs contained, you are wasting your money and could end up spending a whole lot more if your pigs escape and cause damage.

The second-biggest expense is usually the ark. If you have access to barns, stables or even old brick-built pigsties that can house the pigs, this item of equipment will not be necessary. Even if you do not have a suitable building and have limited funds, you can get away with building a straw shelter for your pigs. Although it will not last as long as a purpose-built ark, it should, if built with a framework, last the few months required, until you send your pigs off to the abattoir. You then simply pull it down and build a fresh one for the next batch of weaners. This type of shelter is not suitable, however, if you are living in an urban environment. Straw shelters can look untidy quite quickly once they have been at the mercy of the elements for a while. Even when it is new, your neighbour might find it a less than attractive feature!

Feed and water utensils on the whole are reasonably cheap to buy especially if you shop around, and it is worth spending the money to buy the correct equipment. Buckets and various other containers can be used in the short term, but you will find you will be replacing them every five min-utes due to the rough treatment meted out by the pigs over time.

Some form of handling equipment such as a pig slap board is always useful. For day-to-day use, slap boards are usually made out of a piece of 12-mm plywood 60×60cm (24×24in), with a handhold at the top, and are used in conjunction with a pig stick. They are cheap to buy but many breeders make their own. You can buy plastic ones of similar size as well but these tend to crack if used over a period of time on a day-to-day basis. Some companies also make large, heavy-duty slap boards aimed more at the commercial farmer.

PENS

Some breeds such as the Tamworth are renowned for trying to escape. Pigs have even been known to drop a clod of earth on electric fencing to earth it out so they can dig under the stock fencing in a bid to escape. However, it is unlikely that porkers will worry too much about trying to escape in the short time you will have them. As long as the fencing is sound and they are kept fed and watered, they should give you no trouble.

If you are in an urban area, you will probably have little choice in the size of pen and the area in which you site it, but all pig keepers, whether rural or urban, should try to give their pigs as much space as possible. As a rule of thumb, six pigs can be kept per 0.5 hectares (1 acre). Even if you are an urban pig keeper, your pigs should be given no less than 9×9m (30×30ft).

Unless your land is suffering badly, it is usually unnecessary to rotate the pigs around in the little time you will have them for the freezer. If you are keeping your

Electric fencing is ideal for splitting paddocks into more manageable sections.

pigs as a tool or for breeding, however, or are looking for them to turn over the ground, then it is worth splitting the area into smaller paddocks and rotating the pigs throughout the year. You need to bear in mind, though, that the smaller the area the worse the condition of the pen once the pigs have vacated it. If a pen is too small, this can sometimes lead to boredom and pigs actively looking for a way out.

ESSENTIAL EQUIPMENT

Fencing

Fencing should be strong and secure, with gates sited intelligently and, if possible, with an entrance wide enough for a trailer to fit through. They should open inwards and outwards and, to prevent a boisterous pig lifting the gate off with its snout, one hinge should be placed upside down. If you are in an urban area or conservation area,

you may want to use a wooden gate rather than a metal one. Both do the job but the wooden one looks nicer.

Post and Rail Fencing

Post and rail fencing is by the far the most popular choice for keeping stock contained. If constructed well, it will last for many years. The tanalised posts are usually round and approximately 20cm (8in) in diameter. High-tensile netting is used as a filler between the posts with the bottom of the netting as close to the ground as possible. A rail running around the top, although not necessary, finishes the fencing off nicely. Even in a garden, this type of fencing should be considered over anything else.

Electric Fencing

Many people are reluctant to use electric fencing, especially if they have young children. If this is the case, barbed wire could be considered an alternative. Electric fencing is a useful piece of equipment, however. It is quick and easy to move from field to field and pigs tend to respond to it better. It acts as a deterrent to keep inquisitive pigs from damaging the stock fencing, and, placed along the top of the fence of a boar pen, electric fencing discourages any ideas the boars might have of climbing over. It can also be used to split larger fields into more manageable sections so a system of rotation can be carried out. Commercial farms often manage their pigs in this way, keeping large herds of pigs behind a couple of strands of electric a few inches of the ground, but within the perimeter of an outer stock fence.

Never be tempted to substitute electric fencing for well-constructed stock fencing. Electric fencing on its own would not keep pigs contained indefinitely and the authorities and farmers take a very dim view of loose pigs, more so than any other farm animal.

Checks should be made daily if this type of fencing is used, to ensure that the wire has not shorted out. At least once a week, test the strength of electric being carried along the wire by using a specialist tool. This tool and all other electrical fencing equipment can be bought from your local agricultural store or specialist companies.

Electric fencing is often not necessary. Usually, well-constructed stock fencing should be all that is required to keep a couple of porkers contained for the short time they are with you.

Housing

All pigs need to be protected from the elements by adequate housing, which should be placed in as sheltered position as possible. Traditionally, pigs were kept in purpose-built pigsties, a marketable feature nowadays of many a grand home. For modern-day pig owners, however, there is a variety of housing choices to suit all budgets.

Arks

Traditional wooden and metal pig arks are a popular choice for smallholders or urban pig keepers. Arks come with or without a floor. The type of ark you choose depends on a number of factors:

Budget – an ark with a floor costs considerably more than one without.

Your land – an ark that is placed on free-draining land does not usually require a floor if it is going to be used for just a couple of weaners. On land that holds the water and becomes a quagmire in the winter, you will need an ark with a floor.

The breed of pig you are planning to keep – some of the traditional breeds are not such good 'doers' as others and may benefit more from having a floor.

Your rotation plans – some arks are easier to move than others. If you are planning to rotate the pigs, you will need to move the ark every time, or buy another one. Nowadays arks often come with handholds, loading bars, skids or lifting lugs on top, so that the ark may be lifted by a front loader. Before buying a floored ark, check that it has at least one of these with which to move the ark.

There are a number of other considerations when choosing arks:

Size
The ark must comfortably give your pigs room as they grow. An ark 2.4×1.8m (8×6ft) will accommodate two weaners right up to adult size. If you have limited space, and are keeping one of

For easier cleaning, buy an ark with a removable floor.

the medium-sized breeds such as the Berkshire, you can get away with an ark of 1.8×1.2m (6×4ft), but you could find you do not have enough space in the ark if you run your pigs on for bacon.

Insulation
Some meat producers also have their arks insulated in the belief that a con-stant temperature inside helps porkers gain weight more quickly. If your budget allows, it is certainly worth considering, not only for helping with weight gain, but also for the comfort of the animals. Another way of helping to keep the tem-perature constant is to put old carpet over the roof of the ark. Although it is not pretty to look at, it does keep the inside

of the ark surprisingly warm in winter and cooler in summer.

Ventilation
All shelter should have some form of ventilation to allow a good flow of air. Many ark manufacturers incorporate ventilation at the back as a matter of course but you should try and choose an ark that allows you to regulate the flow of air, rather than just keeping it either open or closed.

Plastic or Wooden?
Plastic can be prone to splitting, so a plastic ark would not be suitable for boisterous boars, although it would be adequate for a couple of pigs. Plastic arks are easy to clean – you simply tip them on their side and steam-clean the inside. Moving them can also be easier than the more traditional ones as most can be rolled around. It is also possible to fit a floor to some plastic arks if this is a requirement.

Wooden arks tend to be difficult to move because of their weight. Although some can be dismantled, moving them is often more bother than it is worth, so a wooden ark is not ideal if the ark needs to be moved on a regular basis. The material blends in better with the surroundings than plastic, but it does need regular attention to preserve the wood, unless it is tanalised.

There are also recycled arks on the market, made from 100 per cent farm waste. If you are concerned about the environment, these are worth considering.

Wooden arks can be difficult to move but they do blend in well with their surroundings.

Traditional Pigsties

The traditional pigsty, a fine sight on the larger country estates in the nineteenth and twentieth centuries, does not compare favourably with today's arks, as it is difficult to clean and has a small entrance. However, as long as it is repaired to a good standard, is as draught-proof as possible and has good ventilation, then there is no reason not to use it if you have access to one.

Straw Shelters

Home-made straw shelters are fine for temporary accommodation and, if built properly, can even last the few months you keep your pigs, without having to undergo major repair. If you live in an urban area, straw shelters are not ideal as they soon start to look untidy after they have been out in the elements, particularly the wind. This type of shelter is often used in woods. Their natural look fits in well with their surroundings and they are protected to a degree from the wind and the rain. Straw shelters are best constructed using large bales over a framework of walls and a roof. If you need to keep the pigs in, you simply place a large bale across the entrance.

Straw shelters are excellent as temporary accommodation.

BUILDING A STRAW SHELTER

Draw the square framework out on paper. Lay down a layer of bales to the required size, leaving a space for the entrance and place a post on the inside of each corner of the shelter. Place a post at each corner of the bale at the entrance and infill with bales until you have reached the desired height. Lining with plywood will prevent the pigs pulling at the straw, and also help to keep the shelter warm inside. Nail the ply on to the poles, making sure there are no nails protruding. For the roof, lay galvanized sheets across the top, making sure they overlap, and finish the shelter by placing large straw bales on top of the sheeting to keep it in place and also to help insulate it. To help protect the inside against driving rain and wind, the sheeting must overhang the shelter.

Bedding

Bedding in some form is necessary, especially if your pig shelter has a hard floor. It protects the pig from injury and keeps it comfortable. Straw is still seen as the cheapest form of bedding for pigs with good insulating properties, although prices can fluctuate wildly depending on the region and the availability. Woodchip is considered the most expensive, with prices differing dramatically again, depending on the grade of shavings. Whichever bedding you use, it should not be skimped on. The more bedding you have in the ark, the longer it seems to stay clean and, of course, the better it keeps the pigs warm and comfortable.

During the summer, if your pigs are in an ark without a floor, it is sometimes better if you dispense with the bedding and allow your pigs to lie on the cool ground. You will often find that they will hollow out a nest within the ark. Even if the ground is rock hard when they first go into the ark, their constant moving and snuffling will reduce the earth to a fine silt, which is quite pleasant for them to lie on.

During wet winters, straw can be used to pile around the entrance of the ark. This helps to reduce the amount of mud that is inevitably dragged in by the comings and goings of the pigs.

Whichever type you decide to use, it should be sweet smelling, fresh and free from dust to encourage the pig to rest in it and to prevent infection.

If you are close to a paper mill and straw is in short supply, it might be possible to come to some arrangement for obtaining shredded paper. Less popular than straw or wood shavings, it makes a good bed nevertheless and is easy to dispose of.

Nowadays there are all types of bedding coming on to the market, including finely cut willow. They all have pros and cons, but most of them are designed for horses, and could therefore work out very expensive if you have quite a few pigs to bed down.

Feeding and Drinking Utensils

Food and water containers should last for many years, but they must be chosen with pigs in mind. Both containers can get rough treatment and inadequate equipment will not last the course. After they have been fed, pigs will often toss the container around looking for that last elusive nut, so it is worth spending that little bit extra in the first place to buy the correct items.

It can be difficult to find a Mexican trough. Farm sales and auction sites on the internet are the best places to get hold of one at a reasonable price.

Troughs

Many smallholders use two troughs, one for water and another for food. Made from steel or rubber and partitioned off into sections, they are easily cleaned and are ideal for two porkers. They can be easily tipped over by snuffling pigs, but placing a trough between two wooden posts will make it more secure. A heavier alternative is the round cast-iron trough, or 'Mexican hat' as it is otherwise known. Split into sections, these troughs can be hard to come by and, because they are attractive to gardeners, can also be quite expensive.

Automatic Drinkers

If you have a good supply of water to the pen, it might be worth considering fitting an automatic drinker. When fitted, the drinker should be checked and cleaned daily to ensure it is not clogged up, and water can run freely. Any pipes leading to the drinkers should be well hidden from inquisitive noses.

Nipple drinkers used widely by indoor herds are not as popular with smallholders as they are with commercial farmers. Unlike the open trough, they tend not to give the pigs a really satisfying drink. Like other automatic drinkers, they should be checked daily for problems.

Buckets

Buckets for carrying feed and water should be strong and durable with handles that are attached securely.

Storage

Although not strictly classed as essential equipment, a dry, vermin-proof building should be available for storing food, bedding, medicines and any spare buckets.

Opposite page: **Vermin-proof metal bins are ideal for storing food.**

If possible, foodstuffs should be kept in a metal bin or some other lidded container, within the building, rather than in the bags in which they are supplied. In any case, food should be kept as far away as possible from anything that might contaminate it. Straw bedding should be placed well away from the food, to prevent spores from the straw infecting the food. If this is not possible, the straw should be kept outside on pallets with a tarpaulin cover over it. Any buckets and feed containers that are kept near the food should be washed before putting away to discourage vermin.

Handling Equipment

If you are keeping just a couple of porkers, you will not need much in the way of handling equipment. A slap board and stick is normally all that is required for moving the pigs around. With adult pigs they are also useful in protecting your body from bites when entering the pen.

Slap Boards

Slap boards, made out of either plastic or wood, are used to direct a pig into a required area. It is placed at the head to encourage the pig to turn away from it, in the desired direction. For a beginner it is not easy co-ordinating the slap board and stick together, to get the pigs to go exactly where you want them to go, so it is worthwhile spending ten minutes each day in the confines of the pen practising moving the pigs around and building up your confidence.

Pig Sticks

Specialist pig sticks, which are used to encourage the pig forward in conjunction with the slap board, can be bought from specialist shops. Like the slap board, how-

A slap board and pig stick are useful tools for moving pigs around.

Noisy beads inside the paddle encourage the pig to move forward.

ever, they are often home-made, while some breeders even use a shepherd's crook.

Paddle

There is now a combined board and stick on the market known as the 'paddle'. Containing beads, the paddle rattles when shaken, encouraging the pig to move forward.

Identification Equipment

It is unlikely that a pig keeper buying in a couple of weaners and keeping them for a few months is going to require any more identification equipment than is sufficient for marking them for the abattoir.

For the purposes of record keeping, pigs can be identified in various ways, such as notching, tagging and tattooing, depending on the breed requirements. A registered weaner will come to you already identified in one of the above ways. Further identification with your herd mark will be required only when it is time to go to the abattoir weeks later. Tagging with a metal tag and/ or slap-marking are the usual ways to identify pigs for this.

If you are worried about tagging pigs for the abattoir, some breeders will tag them for you with your herd number before they come to you. Bear in mind though that the tags could fall out in the intervening period, in which case the pigs would need re-tagging.

Ear Tags and Applicators

Ear tags come in either plastic or metal. Tags used solely for record keeping are normally plastic and tags used for slaughter must be metal, to withstand the scalding process. Make sure the correct applicator is used with the tag.

Slap-Marking Equipment

To ensure they receive the correct carcass back from the abattoir, many smallholders 'slap-mark' the shoulders of their pig. This is like a tattoo, with the herd mark spelt out in pins. Slap-marking kits, which incorporate the slapper, ink and ink box, can be expensive. There are cheaper ones on the market, but they may not be as durable or as simple to handle as other, more expensive versions. Slap-marking is recommended if you are collecting the carcass back. If the abattoir is also going to butcher it for you, it is pointless to slap-mark as you will probably not be able to make out the mark once the carcass has been cut up.

SLAPPING HINTS FOR THE FIRST-TIMER

When new, the ink pad has a thin rubber skin on the inking surface. This has to be punctured to allow absorption of the ink. The easiest way to do this is by going to town with the slapper tattoo pins on the ink box pad.

Taking a spatula or the flat of a knife, force tattoo paste into the pad, but do not over-do it. You now have a pre-inked pad. You will find that the more you use the pad, the better it will become. Re-ink as and when it becomes necessary. If the pad is not used on a weekly basis, wrap it in cling film to prevent drying out, and always reseal the tattoo paste tin after use.

If you are right-handed, stand to the left and far enough back from the pig so that you can reach both shoulders with the head of the slap-marker. If you have many animals to mark, carry the ink box with you in your left hand and slap the pre-inked ink box pad prior to every slap-mark.

If you are at ease with your pigs, you will find that they do not even react to being slapped.

Do not swing the slapper tattoo like a sledgehammer; use a light wrist action. Despite the length of the tattoo pins, providing they are inked well you will need only a light penetration of the skin to leave a good legible mark.

Using ordinary slapper tattoo paste you can satisfactorily slap your pigs up to two weeks prior to slaughter, rather than trying to mark them as you load them all in a rush. Using permanent tattoo paste it is possible to slap-mark your pigs from 10 weeks old using 10mm high characters. The mark will then grow with the animal, so that, by the time it is 10 weeks older, the mark will be the conventional 15mm high and still legible.

Bear in mind that the tattoo paste may be consumed with the meat, and many tattoo pastes contain animal fats obtained outside the EU. Therefore, to prevent any risk of disease contamination, use only a fully synthetic slapper tattoo paste with at least cosmetic grade ingredients.

If you are going to mark only a few animals at a time it is easier and less expensive not to bother with an ink box. Instead, use an old toothbrush to transfer tattoo ink to the tattoo pins. If your animals have dark patches on the shoulders, green ink may be used as an effective alternative to black.

(Courtesy of www.idandtrace.com)

OTHER ITEMS OF EQUIPMENT

Wheelbarrow

A wheelbarrow will be invaluable for carrying sacks of feed around, or when cleaning out arks and pens. Choose a lightweight one that is easy to push, even through mud. Electric wheelbarrows make light work of jobs, but can be hard to negotiate around corners.

Shovels, Forks and Brooms

Choose forks with a slightly curved edge as they tend to pick up straw easier. Brooms should be hard-bristled and not too long-handled, to enable you to sweep out arks. Shovels should be as lightweight as possible.

Disinfectants

You should have at least one disinfectant in your equipment, and preferably two, one powder and one liquid for general use. Powder ones are useful for disinfecting arks or other pig housing once they have been cleaned out. Make sure they are safe to use around animals and always follow the manufacturer's instructions.

Hosepipe

A hosepipe is ideal for hosing down trailers, or for rinsing buckets and other containers. The hose should be kept tidy and away from inquisitive noses. In the winter it is worth building a box around the hose and lagging the tap with insulating material to help prevent freezing.

Trailer

Although not a necessary purchase straight away, it is always useful to have your own trailer rather than borrowing one. However, this can be quite a significant outlay so you should consider buying one only if you are sure that pig keeping is for you.

There are many decent second-hand trailers on the market and if possible you should choose a trailer that is fully enclosed and not too big, but large enough for two pigs to turn around in. The ramp should be at a shallow angle, otherwise you may find that the pigs are reluctant to load.

Miscellanous Items

When starting out, it is often the small, forgotten items that make life easier. These need not necessarily be expensive but they often turn out to be a godsend. A good place to keep them is in the pockets of the coat that is always worn when 'doing' the pigs. Failing that, they should be kept in a 'tidy' box, preferably the type of container that is used for carrying horse-grooming equipment.

Torch
Choose a head torch so that, if you have to carry out a job in the dark, you will have both hands free.

String or Baler Twine
String or twine is always useful in tying up broken gates, or other emergencies.

Pocket Knife
You should always carry a knife, which should be attached to a used coloured bobbin. The bobbin will help you locate the knife if it falls out of your pocket into straw or the pen.

Everything should be in place before the pigs arrive.

Horse Brush

Pigs can suffer from dry skin, so a good weekly brush with a horse brush not only benefits their skin but also gives them great pleasure!

Pig Weighing Band

These are useful for obtaining the approximate weight of your pig. They work just like a tape measure and give a fairly good indication of the pig's weight.

Clothes

Even when you keep just a couple of pigs, it does not take long for your clothes to get that 'piggy' smell. It is a good idea therefore to invest in some waterproof trousers and a jacket that can be worn when working with them. Waterproof trousers can be bought from agricultural merchants and their prices vary depending on the thickness of the rubber.

TAKING DELIVERY

Preparation for your pigs should not be a last-minute effort. Ideally, you should have fencing and the required equipment in place at least a week or so before the arrival of your pigs. This allows you to have a thorough last check to ensure that everything is how it should be. Bear in mind that, when the pigs arrive, they should be kept as quiet as possible for the first few days to enable them to settle down. Their ark should be placed in as quiet a corner as possible, away from curious dogs and other situations that might be stressful for them.

Make sure you have enough manpower on the day to enable a smooth delivery. If you are in an urban area, everything should be done to minimize the chance of the pigs escaping on to the road. Children, neighbours and anyone else who is eager to visit the pigs should be kept away for the first week or until the pigs are familiar with their new surroundings. You should receive a bag of food with your weaners to enable you to change their food over slowly to the brand you will be using. If possible, ask the breeder for details of their food, and try and keep them on the same brand of food. Moving to a new situation is very stressful for weaners and they can suffer from an upset stomach. Keeping to the same food means that they have to deal with one less change.

CHAPTER 4

Training and Information

PIG COURSES

Like any new venture, it pays to do the research and be as prepared as possible, before embarking on what could be, in this case, a life-changing experience. Pigs are relatively easy to look after but, inevitably, the more knowledge you have, the better the job you will do and the easier it will be.

Pigs can be unruly and no amount of reading will prepare you properly for keeping them. Only a hands-on experience, and hearing first-hand from other pig keepers, will really give you a feel of what is involved.

Pig day courses over the last few years have grown immensely in popularity, as more and more people are looking to keep pigs. They are a fantastic way of handling the different breeds and gaining an insight into their different characters. At the moment, however, there are no regulations in force for running a pig course. Courses can be run in any way the breeder sees fit and he can charge whatever people

A pig course is recommended before embarking on pig keeping.

Check that the breeder from whom you buy your weaners is happy to help should you have a problem.

will pay. Consequently, courses are now available all over the country, as breeders look at ways to bring in extra money. Normally, pig courses last all day, covering the basics required to keep pigs, as well as breed from them. The price usually includes lunch and refreshments and often you will be given course work to take home with you.

Information on courses can be found on the internet and the various smallholder magazines that are on sale. When choosing a course, try to go on recommendation from friends and acquaintances. Before booking, check with the breeder exactly what the course entails and how much of it is hands-on.

THE BREEDER

Most breeders of repute care where their weaners go and will offer a free advice service to new owners if required, once the pigs have left their care. This can be invaluable to the first-time pig keeper so, when buying pigs, you should feel confident that you are able to ring the breeder for advice in the event of any problems. Do not buy pigs from any breeder who appears to be glad to get rid of them and you. If there is a problem in the future, they may not welcome your telephone calls.

If you are having problems sourcing a breeder, the British Pig Association, as well as the relevant breed club, normally has a list of breeders who have stock for sale.

Agricultural shows with pig classes are also worth visiting as sometimes breeders who are showing their pigs will also be advertising weaners for sale.

THE BREED SOCIETY

Most of the traditional breeds have a club or society that you are able to join for a few pounds a year, even if you are not yet keeping pigs. This is an excellent way of meeting like-minded people who are more often than not willing to help you if you have a problem. Most clubs organize workshops and trips throughout the year and social events are often held in the summer.

Clubs are always looking for members to get involved in the running of the club so there is often an opportunity to sit on

the committee and play more of an active role once you have been with them for a while.

THE BRITISH PIG ASSOCIATION

If you are buying birth notified pedigree stock, you will probably have heard of the British Pig Association (BPA). The herd books of all British traditional breeds, with the exception of the British Lop, are held by the BPA. The Association website contains a wealth of information as well as up-to-date government information on rules and regulations that might affect pig keepers. It also has a very useful database of breeders as well as listing stock for sale. Although membership is primarily aimed at breeders, there is the possibility in the

Breed societies often organize trips to other farms.

Agricultural shows are an ideal way of seeing all the breeds in one area.

future of bringing in a membership that is aimed specifically for the person keeping just a couple of pigs.

SMALLHOLDERS' CLUBS

Most counties run a smallholders' club, with the exception of Scotland and Wales. These clubs are an excellent way of meeting people reasonably close by, who share similar interests. Trips and workshops are held regularly as are social events. Currently Scotland has just two clubs that cater for pig keepers: the Scottish Smallholders' Association, which covers the whole of Scotland, and the Deanbank Smallholders' Group, covering South-West Scotland. In Wales, it is the Wales and Border Counties Pig Breeders' Association. Every year this association puts on a hugely successful pig show as part of the Royal Welsh and Smallholders' Show in Builth Wells. They also run numerous workshops, trips and social events as well as publishing a very useful directory and other booklets.

FORUMS

Smallholding forums are an incredibly useful way of accessing information quickly if you have a problem. Once you have registered, which is usually free, you are able to post questions and these are normally responded to within hours. Forums are excellent for hearing the views and opinions of pig keepers all over the UK as well as further afield. Many experienced breeders take part in forums so you are just as likely to receive comments from an experienced breeder as from another novice. Most forums are independent but some are attached to magazines and current rural programmes.

Sometimes, it turns out that other users on the forum live quite close to one another and friendships can be formed between smallholders who would never have met otherwise.

BOOKS AND MAGAZINES

The increase in pig keeping and smallholding in general has led to a good choice in books and magazines being published. Some smallholder magazines are geared towards a particular hobby, such as poultry, and you should choose carefully the magazines that suits your needs.

AGRICULTURAL SHOWS

Visiting agricultural shows is an extremely pleasurable way of learning about the different breeds and at least one show should be visited before embarking on keeping pigs. Not only do you have practically every breed in one area, but also pig breeders from all over the country are on hand to spend time answering your questions and talking to you once their showing classes are finished for the day.

CHAPTER 5

Rules and Regulations

THE IMPORTANCE OF RECORD KEEPING

Pigs are classed as farm animals, so, whether you are keeping one pig as a pet or a whole herd for meat, you must have certain things in place before you take them on. Some records are required by law and must be sent to the relevant government departments. Others you should keep for your own benefit. All records should be kept up to date and filled in precisely. In addition, they should be made available for inspection on request by the Local Authority.

If you do not have in place paperwork that is required by law, you run the risk of prosecution and could be fined thousands of pounds.

All pig owners are advised to look at the Defra UK website from time to time for up-to-date information.

PAPERWORK

Holding Number

Before you allow pigs to come on to your property, you must obtain a Holding Number for them. This number allows the government to trace all livestock in the event of a disease outbreak. A Holding Number, or CPH for short, is a nine-digit number representing the county and parish of the holding, as well as a unique number given to you, for example

32/530/0066 (county 32/parish 530/unique number 0066).

CPH numbers are easy to obtain. In most cases a form will be sent out, filled in and sent back, and number will usually arrive by post a week or so later. In Scotland, a digital map of the property sometimes has to be sent before a number is issued. This can be obtained from the Rural Land Registry (RLR). Your CPH should be applied for at least a month before the pigs are due to arrive. This allows for any problems obtaining your number to be ironed out.

If you live in Scotland, you should apply to the local office of the Scottish Government Rural Payments and Inspections Directorate for your number. In Wales, it is the Divisional Office of the Welsh Assembly and in England, the Rural Payments Agency (RPA).

Herd Number

Once you have received your Holding Number and your pigs have arrived, you should apply for a Herd Number from your local Animal Health Licensing Office. This is easier than applying for a CPH number; in many cases, it is given over the telephone and a hard copy is sent on a few days later. This number is just as important as the

Opposite page: **You must have a Holding Number in place before you take receipt of your pigs.**

CPH and, when you receive it, you will also find movement forms, a medical record book and other useful information on the care of your pigs in the same envelope.

The Herd Number is made up of two letters and four digits. The letters identify the county and the numbers are unique to you. As this number is a means of identifying your pigs, any pig over 12 months of age must be clearly identified with it whenever the animal goes off the property. Animals going to slaughter under this age must also be identified with the Herd Number.

Movement Licence

No pig is allowed to be moved without a licence accompanying it. Even if it is just down the road, if it is moving to another holding, a movement form must be filled in and sent to the relevant department within three days. Exceptions to this are fields that belong to you but are not adjoining your property, and are within an 8-km (5-mile) radius of the Holding Number address. All movement details should then be recorded in a movement book.

In England, the form comes in quadruple and requires you to fill in the following details (the required information for Scottish and Welsh movement forms is slightly different and not so in-depth):

- dates of travel (departure and arrival);
- loading and unloading times;
- departure CPH;
- arrival CPH;
- name and address of premises of departure;
- name and address of premises of arrival;
- details and number on animals being transported;
- haulier details.

A copy should be kept by yourself and another should be sent to Trading Standards within three days of the movement. The other two copies should either be given to the relevant people or again kept by yourself if appropriate.

A twenty-day standstill will automatically be triggered once a pig has arrived on your property. This must be strictly adhered to and no pig is allowed to leave your property within this time unless they are going straight to slaughter. If you have another pig come on during that time, the twenty-day standstill starts all over again.

IDENTIFICATION

Defra accepts four ways of identifying your pig:

1 Ear tag – an ear tag must be stamped or printed, not handwritten. It must have your Herd Number on, preceded by 'UK'. Tags used for slaughter must be metal to withstand the carcass processing. Tags used for general movement or record keeping can be plastic.
2 Tattoo – a tattoo of your herd mark is usually used on light-coloured pigs, such as the Middle White or Tamworth. Gloucester Old Spots can also be tattooed if they have light-coloured ears. 'UK' in front of the herd mark is not needed when tattooing.
3 Slap-mark – this permanent ink mark detailing your herd mark is applied on one or both shoulders of the pig. There is a knack to slap-marking so that the number is legible, and your slap-marking technique will improve with practice.
4 Temporary mark – a pig can be identified with a paint mark, for example, a red line or blue circle. It must last until

Ears must be tagged with a metal tag for slaughtering.

the pig reaches its destination and must be combined with the movement document. A temporary mark may be used only for pigs under 12 months of age moving from holding to holding. When going to slaughter or to market, pigs must be identified by ear tag, tattoo or slap-marking.

MEDICAL RECORDS

You will receive a medical record book with the hard copy of your Herd Number. All medicines administered (including wormers) must be recorded within 72 hours and kept for at least three years. The following information is required:

- which animals were given the treatment and their identification number
- the date they were treated, and the date treatment finished
- the name of the product and the batch number
- end of withdrawal period date
- the name of the person who administered the treatment.

FURTHER RECORD KEEPING

General

Once a year you need to record the maximum number of pigs normally present on the holding.

Slap-marking your pig before it goes to the abattoir is recommended, to ensure that your carcass can be identified.

Financial Records

If you are working to a budget, it is vital to keep a record of the money that is being spent. Food is one of the biggest outlays and a close eye should be kept on this cost. The price of pig food seems to be going up and up and it is worth shopping around if you seem to be exceeding your budget in this area.

Breed Registration Records

If you are a member of an association such as the British Pig Association, you will be required to keep a record of all your registered pigs, even if you only have two, and their identification number, and every year you will be ask to update these records. Nowadays changes to records can be done online.

DEFRA DO'S AND DON'TS

By law, there are certain guidelines to which you have to adhere. The following has been taken from the Defra website, www.defra.gov.uk.

It is illegal to feed any pig any catering waste (including used cooking oil) from restaurants, kitchens (both household and central), and other catering facilities even if those establishments cater solely for vegetarians.

Current legislation also imposes strict controls banning the feeding of other materials of animal origin or products containing them to farmed animals.

There is however a small number of exceptions to this and the following materials may be fed to pigs:

Liquid milk or colostrum may be fed to pigs kept on the same holding as that on which the milk or colostrum originated;

Former foodstuffs (Other than catering waste food from kitchens, catering facilities, etc) containing rennet, melted fat, milk or eggs, but where these materials are not the main ingredient;

Restricted proteins such as fishmeal, (animal-derived) di-calcium or tri-calcium phosphate, or blood products if suitably processed;

Milk, milk products and white water sourced from registered premises, or as former foodstuffs from retail outlets;

These products must not enter the kitchens or they become catering waste.

It is permissible to source certain types of former foodstuffs (*see above*), as well as

fruit and vegetables, from non-catering premises for feeding to pigs, but this must only be done from those premises that either do not handle materials banned from being fed to pigs, or that have procedures in place to ensure complete separation from prohibited materials, and these procedures have been agreed with the local authority.

Do not be tempted to feed catering waste food or other types of banned material to your pigs. This is illegal. Contaminated waste food can spread viruses and bacteria and, when infected with a disease such as Foot and Mouth, pigs can quickly infect other animals. As long as you follow the rules and regulations, you will help keep your animals healthy and reduce the risk of future outbreaks of disease.

All pigs need to be recorded once a year.

CHAPTER 6

Looking After Your Pigs

KEEPING TO A ROUTINE

Like any animal, pigs thrive on routine. It settles them and allows them to lead a stress-free life. Routine also helps build a trusting relationship between you and your animals, as well as helping to prevent bullying if you have a few pigs living together.

Haphazard feeding and watering leads to stress and, if you are raising pigs for the freezer, this stress could lead to loss of weight, or the pigs not reaching the required weight as quickly as they should. So, as far as possible, you should try to feed them at the same times every day, although you should not worry to much if on the odd occasion you miss a feed, or feed later than usual. The occasional slight deviation from their routine will not affect them too badly.

As a general rule, depending on your set-up, to feed, water and do a general check of your pigs should not take any more than twenty minutes of your time in the morning and in the evening. If your

Pigs must be fed at the same time every day.

Take time out of each day to establish a bond with your pigs.

pigs are on your doorstep and everything is to hand, it can take even less time.

DAILY JOBS

Ideally, pigs should be fed twice a day. In the wild, pigs eat little and often. They spend their days foraging, rarely going without food for too long. When they are not foraging, they are sleeping. Unless your pigs are kept ranging freely in a wood where foods such as nuts, roots, and so on, are plentiful, it is almost impossible to emulate this way of life for them. Most pigs, especially those kept in an urban setting, rely solely on their keeper for food, and this should be borne in mind when looking to keep pigs. By feeding them

twice a day, you ensure that they are not going too long without food. It also gives you the chance to do a quick health check each time. Although they are very rarely ill, when something is wrong, pigs can go down very quickly. Checking them twice a day will enable you to pick up on problems immediately.

Feeding and watering utensils should be cleaned regularly; at the very least they should be rinsed out once a day. In winter, utensils can become caked in mud surprisingly quickly and, if fresh food is tipped on to the mud, you are running the risk of the pigs picking up an infection as they eat. Ideally, in wet weather, troughs and buckets should be regularly moved to a different spot in the pen, to prevent the area around the trough becoming too poached.

Automatic drinking bowls should be wiped clean and fittings checked. Clean, fresh water encourages the pigs to drink frequently, which is especially important in the summer months.

Nipple drinkers should not be the first choice for someone keeping just a couple of pigs as they do not seem to give the pigs the same satisfying drink as they get when drinking from a trough. If nipple drinkers are used, they must be thoroughly checked every day. Sometimes limescale can build up and restrict the flow of water getting to the pig, and over time this can have serious consequences.

It is very easy to forget or not to bother to check the interior of the shelter daily. When you look through the doorway from a distance and all seems well, why should you bother bending down and checking the whole of the inside? In fact, pigs often chew the interior of their arks, loosening nails or screws in the process, so a couple of minutes daily just running your eyes over the interior for any problems might save you money in the long term. You can also check at the same time that the bedding does not need replacing or the pigs have not suddenly started using a corner of the ark as a toilet, which sometimes happens, especially in particularly cold or wet weather. Even if your pigs are kept in a barn or stable, you should still give the inside of the building a daily once-over. Pigs love old buildings, especially brick ones, and will give old bricks their full attention until one falls out. Once this happens, it is only a matter of time before others fall out, weakening the walls.

Electric fencing is only effective if it is working, so checking it daily is a must. Obstructions such as stones, long grass or clods of earth lying across it can result in the wire shorting out. Pigs very quickly learn that, if they push stones or earth across the wire, they are then able to push under the wire to escape without fear of been 'shocked'. Once a week, the strength of the electric current being carried along the wire should be measured with a suitable tool.

On the whole, pigs are usually very healthy. You would be very unlucky to have a pig fall ill in the short time they are with you. However, it is still worth giving your pigs a daily mini health check, so that any potential problem can be sorted early and the relevant action taken.

Start at the head and run your eyes and hands over both sides of their body, paying particular attention to any small cuts. Usually, cuts heal themselves without any problem. Occasionally, though, they will open up and turn quite nasty, so it is worth spraying any cut, no matter how small, with a suitable antiseptic.

Stand back and look at the general demeanour of the pigs. Do they look happy or are they looking tucked up? Are they walking properly or do they appear stiff? Is their skin healthy-looking or do they have rough red patches, which could be a sign of mange or lice? Do not panic if a pig does not seem quite itself; like humans, pigs have off days too. Just keep a very close eye on things and, if in doubt, ring the vet.

WEEKLY JOBS

It is surprising what pigs unearth once they start rooting. Pens that appear to be free from debris when the pigs first go in will suddenly throw up the most amazing things. Stones are brought to the surface, along with bottles, pieces of wire and other alien objects. A weekly pen check must therefore be carried out to ensure that dangerous objects are removed.

During the spring and summer, plants

Your pigs will appreciate a good rub and an oiling.

and flowers found growing in the pen should be checked to ensure they are not poisonous. If in doubt, the plant should be pulled up and burnt. Do not pull it up and leave it lying in the pen as some plants can be more dangerous when drying out than they can while growing.

MONTHLY JOBS

Arks should be given a thorough cleaning once a month, and more often if the pen gets muddy. This job should be carried out even in summer to minimize infection. If possible, the ark should be then sprayed with a disinfectant that is safe to use around animals. Straw should be burnt or put on the compost heap.

If you are sending your pigs to the abattoir at five or six months, worming is not necessary. The pigs should have come to you already wormed and this should last them until it is time to go. However, if you are keeping them on longer for bacon, they will need worming at six months. Wormers can be bought over the internet or from your local vet and are usually given either as an injection or in their water or food. Injection is best, as the pig is guaranteed to get the full quota. Putting it in the feed, even if you split the pigs up so they each have their own wormer, does not guarantee that they will consume all the powder.

THE FUN JOBS

Pigs love being around humans and they like nothing better than a good scratch and a belly rub. Handling them daily and getting them used to your voice also helps make life easier when the time comes to load them up for the trip to the abattoir.

Once a week, give your pigs a good exfoliation and oiling. Not only does this keep their skin in good condition but it also helps to build up a bond between you.

You can buy specialist pig oil from agricultural merchants, but, as it is a by-product of the petroleum industry, you may prefer to use a gentler product such as baby oil. A horse-grooming brush is fantastic for taking off the loose dry skin prior to oiling.

GENERAL UPKEEP

Every effort should be made to keep the area around the pigs tidy and professional-looking. This is especially important if you are living in an urban area. A garden with pigs should still look like a garden, not a farm. The combination of rain and pigs usually leads to mud, so if you are in an urban area, try and keep your pigs through the summer. If you do experience a wet summer, and your pen becomes like a quagmire, make an extra effort to keep the area around the pen mud-free and tidy.

Bales of straw should ideally be kept hidden in a shed, or stored in a basic shelter that you have built. If this is not possible, cover it neatly with a tarpaulin that does not flap wildly in the wind. Rake any loose straw up daily so that it does not blow into next door's garden. Water should be kept as clean as possible and any food left by the pigs should be cleared up so as not to encourage rats. Vermin lead to the majority of complaints about pigs kept in an urban area. As rats and mice are often prevalent around houses, food left lying will bring them in in droves. Even if you live in the countryside, be sensible about how you store the food.

If you ensure that your pigs do not become an eyesore, your neighbours will be less likely to complain.

Keep the area where your pigs live as tidy as possible.

CHAPTER 7

Feeding for the Freezer

Keeping a couple of pigs for the freezer has become quite fashionable over the past few years. Many people start out by keeping chickens, and see pig keeping as a natural progression towards their dream of a degree of self-sufficiency. Fuelled by newspaper articles and television programmes, there is now a growing realization that pigs can be kept almost anywhere on a reasonably sized plot. This, coupled with an increased interest in the source and taste of food, has seen a significant rise in the numbers of pigs being kept.

MEAT QUALITY

Most people start pig keeping with the idea of filling their freezer with joints, sausages and bacon, but this is only a fraction of what can be produced from a carcass. Even if you are quite happy with joints and a few sausages, and no more, it is still important to feed your pig correctly from day one, to help you get the best from it in the way of fat content, taste and texture.

The very fact that you are thinking about keeping a couple of pigs for the

Your own home-produced pork will taste far superior to anything you can buy in the supermarket.

Tamworths make superb bacon pigs.

freezer means you care about what goes into the production of the meat that you eat. Research has shown that even the most expensive pork from a supermarket can lack the depth of taste of meat from a home-produced pig. This is one reason for the growth in popularity of farmers' markets, as more and more consumers turn their backs on mass-produced pork, preferring meat that has more taste and has been produced locally. Many supermarkets have identified the growing market for pork from traditional English breeds, and offer products from these breeds, supposedly kept free-range. Often, however, all is not always as it seems. Pretty pictures on the packaging give the shopper the impression that they are buying pure traditional breed pork and that, by buying the meat, they are helping to preserve the breeds. This is often just a marketing

ploy and the meat is more likely to be the result of a traditional breed crossed with a commercial one, although this is not made completely clear unless you take the time to read the small print. The fact is that it is simply not commercially viable for supermarkets to cater to the masses using slow-growing pure traditional breeds and, in any case, that meat may be too fatty for many tastes.

Fat

Historically there are three types of pig: the lard pig, the bacon pig such as the Tamworth, and the pork pig, such as a Berkshire or Middle White. Even though carcasses from each of the three types will be different, all of them will have a relatively thick layer of fat. Even one of the leaner breeds, such as the Oxford Sandy and Black, will have a good layer of fat in comparison with the carcasses of commercially produced pigs such as the Landrace.

Nowadays it is widely recognized that a layer of fat on meat is critical to its taste. Without it, the meat would be bland and dry. In the 1970s, however, things were different. Many traditional British breeds were in grave danger of becoming extinct due to the demand for leaner meat that could be produced more economically. Hardly anyone wanted meat from the fattier breeds and some, such as the Lincolnshire Curly Coat and the Cumberland, were indeed lost for ever. The determination of a small band of breeders saved a number of other breeds until, in 1973, the Rare Breed Survival Trust was formed and took the survivors under its wing. The decline was halted and, in the last few years, many of the breeds that were once on the verge of extinction have prospered due to the recognition of the quality of the meat that they produce.

Although it is important to feed your pigs so that they develp that layer of fat, too much fat can be off-putting, and therefore it is imperative that they are not overfed. Ideally, you want to be aiming for a minimum of half an inch back fat and not more than three-quarters of an inch.

Until you develop a practised eye for their condition, pigs should be weighed regularly, using either the weight formula or the weight tape measure, up to two or three weeks before they go. Their back should also be checked regularly using the condition scoring. On average they should be putting on no more than a quarter to half a kilo a week.

Pigs should be allowed to indulge in their natural instinct of rooting.

Other Factors

There are many other factors that determine the quality and taste of the end result, particularly the food that the pig eats and the way in which it is kept. However, giving it the correct food and allowing it to live a stress-free natural life is no guarantee of the best-tasting meat, although you will still have better-tasting meat than you can buy in the supermarket.

Research has also shown that different bloodlines of the same breed play a part in determining the quality of the meat and the size of the cuts. Two different bloodlines of Berkshires, for example, raised and cooked in the same way, can taste and look totally different. Only by raising different bloodlines over a period of time will you actually start to pick up on the difference.

Pigs should have access to grass and soil and be able to carry out their natural instinct of rooting. Not only does rooting occupy the pigs during the day and keep them from mischief, but also what they root up and eat all helps towards the end taste. Pigs without either of the above will never acquire a really succulent taste.

If you are lucky to have woods containing acorns, or other types of nuts, these can have a wonderful effect on the taste of the meat. However, the pigs should not be allowed to gorge too many at one time as the tannic acid in the acorns can cause stomach problems.

There should always be a good supply of fresh water in the pig pens. If possible, pigs should have sufficient access to water in a container that allows them to have a properly satisfying drink. For this reason, a trough or bucket should be used rather than automatic drinkers.

FEED

Organic or GM-Free

In an ideal world, all breeders would feed organically and, if your budget can stand it, this is definitely the way to go. After

Pigs must have access to sufficient water.

The easiest way of feeding is to buy compound food.

all, probably one of the main reasons why you are raising your own food is to ensure that what you are eating is as free from chemicals and other 'nasties' as possible. However, feeding organically can make quite a considerable difference to your final feed bill, and as this bill will already take quite a chunk of your budget (usually 70–80 per cent of the total cost of producing the pig), it may not be financially viable.

The next best thing to organic is to buy compound food that does not contain genetically modified (GM) crops or growth enhancers. Some mills or agricultural merchants do not sell GM-free food and, if they do, they often sell GM food as well. It is important therefore to check the label carefully on the bag before purchasing.

Finding, Purchasing and Storing Supplies

Do not wait until your pigs have arrived before you go searching for agricultural merchants. Sometimes, especially if you live in a middle of a suburb, finding one within a reasonable distance can be diffi-

cult and not all sell pig food, although they should be able to get some in for you.

If you are lucky enough to have a couple of feed suppliers nearby, it is worth comparing their prices. Even a few pence difference will count.

Compound food usually comes in either 20 or 25kg bags. If you have the space to store food, you should consider buying in bulk. Two weaners will need approximately half a tonne of food from 8 weeks to 6 months, so, to save money, it is worth shopping around for the best price then negotiating on a price for it to be delivered. You can save even more if you pick the food up yourself rather than having it delivered.

The bags should be stored on pallets and any opened bags should be tipped into a vermin proof bin to prevent contamination and to keep it as fresh as possible.

Compound Food or Mixing Your Own?

If they are fed compound food, your pigs will be receiving a balanced diet without the fuss of putting together your own mix. There are various types suitable for all

A close eye must be kept on the weight of your pigs.

stages of growth and you should be careful to choose the correct type for your pigs.

Many experienced breeders make up their own mix, which is far cheaper than buying compound food. For the beginner, though, this is not recommended. Unless you know exactly what you are doing and have developed a good eye for conditioning and weight gain on a pig, you could find that you are feeding totally inappropriate amounts, resulting in underweight or overweight pigs. You would also need considerably more space in which to store the different grains.

Types of Food

Feeding your pigs should not be allowed to become complicated, which can so easily happen if you seek advice from too many people. No two breeders will give you the same advice. What works for them will not necessarily work for someone else. There are many factors involved as to how well the pigs will do on a particular type of food, including the weather, their level of activity, the breed of pig and its age and weight.

The types of compound food available for pigs are as follows:

Creep food – very small pellets containing protein of at least 18 per cent, usually given ad lib to piglets from three weeks onwards.

Grower – slightly larger than creep food and high in protein. Grower should be fed with caution as it can result in the pigs getting too fat too quickly. Sometimes called 'finisher'.

Sow and weaner nuts – ideal for the in-pig sow and a sow feeding piglets. Useful for feeding to porkers (pigs brought on for meat).

Ordinary pig nuts – large nuts, usually fed to dry sows and boars. Low protein, so not really suitable for porkers.

Meal – must always be fed wet to prevent choking. However, there is a tendency for pigs to gulp this type of food and perhaps choke. Mash will often get a sick pig eating again, especially if you add molasses.

Unlike commercial breeds, slow-growing traditional breeds tend to lay down back fat far more quickly if a watchful eye is not kept on their weight. Attempting to push them on by over-feeding will result in a fatty carcass and little meat. Traditional breeds are not meant to be treated in this way.

The easiest and least complicated system therefore is to feed sow and weaner nuts from when the pigs arrive to when they go. These have enough protein (usually 12–18 per cent) to help growth, but not enough to put too much fat on unless you drastically over-feed. Whichever type you decide to feed, it should be introduced gradually.

AMOUNTS TO FEED

Working out how much to feed your pigs is often a case of trial and error. Pigs on the whole love their food and will eat almost everything that is put in front of them. Some breeds such as the Gloucester Old Spot have a tendency to gain back fat rather quickly. Other breeds, such as the Tamworth, are leaner and can require more food to bring them up to the desired weight. However, caution should also be exercised with the Tamworth, if you are keeping them on longer for bacon. Even the lean Tamworth can end up gaining too much back fat after about six months if you are not careful with the amounts that you feed.

It is very difficult to specify definitive amounts to feed pigs. A good starting

CONDITION SCORE

Every pig is different and gauging their condition is really about developing an eye and a feel for it. The following will enable you to get an idea as to what condition your pigs are in:

Condition Score	Definition
Emaciated	Bones clearly visible
Thin	Bones can be felt without pressure when palm of hand is laid flat on skin
Ideal	Bones can be felt only with firm pressure when palm of hand is laid flat on skin
Fat	Bones can be felt only when fingertips are pressed into skin
Obese	No bones felt

point is to give each pig 450g (1lb) of food, split into two meals a day for every month of age, up to a maximum of 2.25kg (5lb). For example a three-month-old weaner should be on approximately 1.5kg (3lb) of food a day.

Once you have reached the 2.25kg (5lb) mark, the pigs should be maintained on this amount until they are ready to go. If you feel your pigs are losing or gaining too much weight, you should change the amount accordingly. If you find your pigs have become fatter than you intended, cutting back on the food three to four weeks before they go will often sort things out. Some breeders automatically cut back on the pigs' rations a month before they go to prevent too much back fat being laid down.

In particularly wet or cold weather, weight loss may be prevented by increasing rations.

ADDITIONAL FOODSTUFFS

Fruit and Vegetables

The compound food should be bulked up with as much vegetable and fruit as possible, as this will add a wonderful succulence and taste to the meat. It also prevents the pigs getting bored with their food and losing their appetite – this can happen, even with a pig! Some vegetables such as parsnips can cause skin lesions and should be avoided.

By law, in order to prevent cross-contamination, you are not allowed to feed any foodstuff that has passed through your kitchen. Your green food therefore must come from another source. If you have a surplus of vegetables from your vegetable garden or off your fruit trees, throw them to the pigs. Vegetables and fruit from a vegetable market are also quite safe to be used as long as this is all they are selling. Potato must always be cooked and given in small pieces so that it is easily digestible. Also prohibited are catering waste, food that might have come in contact with meat products and meat itself.

It is also possible to feed milk and milk-based products, biscuits, bakery waste and pasta. Products that contain certain ingredients, such as rennet or melted fat, milk or eggs, can also be fed to livestock, as long as they are not the main ingredient in those products. If you are planning to feed any of the above, you must check with your local Animal Licensing Authority as to whether you have to be registered as a user. Checking the Defra website from time to time for any changes in the law regarding feeding is also important.

Milk should be fed with caution as it can cause diarrhoea if consumed in large quantities. Pigs do love it, however, and many people are of the opinion that it can give the meat extra succulence.

READY TO GO

Unless you particularly want to take your pigs on longer for bacon, they should be ready to go at approximately six months and at an approximate weight of 55–60kg (120–130lb).

It is not essential to keep a pig longer for bacon. It is perfectly possible to get superb-tasting bacon off a six-month-old porker, and the only difference will be smaller slices. Should you decide to take the pig on for another two or three months, a careful eye must be kept on its weight. Very often pigs get to a certain age and, rather than keep growing, they simply pile on the pounds.

WEIGHT-MEASURING FORMULA

1 Measure the length of the pig from the root of the tail to a point in between its ears in inches.
2 Measure the girth around the shoulders, keeping the tape tight up to the front legs.
3 Multiply the length by the girth.
4 Divide that number by 13 for a lean pig, 12 for a medium pig and 11 for a fat pig.
5 The answer gives you an approximation of the weight of the pig in pounds.

For example:
Length 40in × Girth 30in = 1200
1200 divided by 12 for a medium pig = 100lb

If you are unsure about your pig's weight, the formula above can help you measure a pig to find its live-weight. Alternatively you can buy a specialist weight tape measure, which will give you an indication of the weight of your pig.

CATEGORIES FOR MEAT PRODUCTION

There are a number of stages in the life of a pig being kept for meat production. The weights given below indicate what you need to work towards.

Suckling pig – usually under eight weeks and weighing around 15kg. Its popularity has increased over the last few years, especially with the restaurant trade. Today, prices for suckling pigs are quite exorbitant.

Weaners – newly weaned pigs between eight and ten weeks and weighing around 20kg. Very popular with smallholders wishing to fatten the pigs themselves. Often sold to finishing units to fatten for the commercial trade.

Porkers – usually around 5–6 months old and weighing approximately 55kg.

Cutters – pork pigs that have been kept on longer than porkers. Usually around nine months of age and weighing around 65kg.

Baconers – pigs such as the Tamworth, grown on specifically for bacon. Usually between nine and twelve months old and weighing around 80kg.

Sausage pigs – pigs used specifically for sausages tend to be older sows or pigs that are no longer required. Because of their age, they can weigh several hundred kilos. Some abattoirs will not take pigs this big; if they do, the cost goes up considerably.

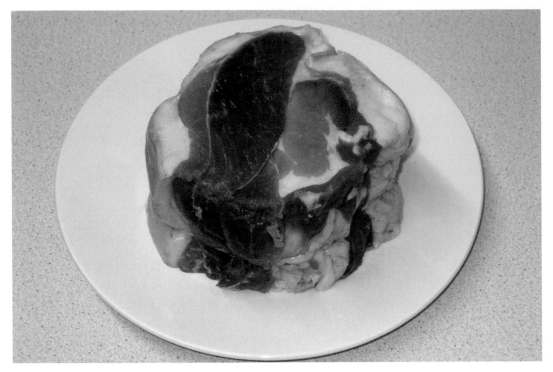

A good layer of fat makes all the difference to the taste of the meat.

THE END RESULT

Do not be too despondent if the meat you receive back from the butcher in your early days is too fat. Keeping pigs for the freezer is really a case of trial and error. Even breeders who have been producing pork for years do not always get it right. The meat will still be the most delicious meat you will ever taste and, as for the fat, you can always trim it away before putting the joint in the oven.

CHAPTER 8

First Aid for Your Pigs

HEALTHY WEANERS

It is very rare for traditional breeds to fall ill, especially in the short time they will be with you. They are known for their hardiness and, as long as they are given shelter and enough food, and are allowed plenty of exercise and fresh air, you would be very unlucky to have any serious problems.

Your weaners should come to you in the peak of health and wormed. Before you take receipt of the pigs they should be checked over. They should have a shiny coat with no dry or red skin and certainly should be free from skin problems such as lice. They should be alert, and move without stiffness or limping. If, on receiving your pigs, you feel that all is not well, do not hesitate to convey your concerns to the breeder. On no account should you accept pigs with which you are not 100 per cent happy. Once you have parted with your money, you could encounter difficulties in sorting out any problems.

Weaners should come to you in the peak of health.

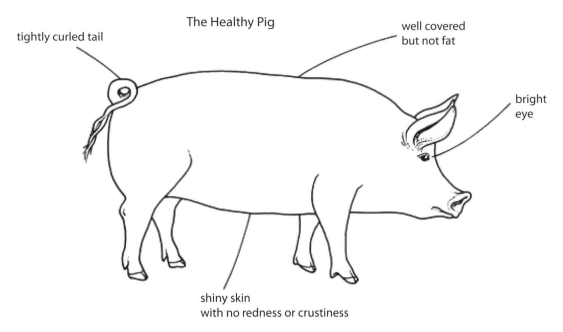

The Healthy Pig

tightly curled tail

well covered
but not fat

bright
eye

shiny skin
with no redness or crustiness

Check that weaners are healthy before buying them.

SIGNS OF ILL HEALTH

Once you have had your pigs for a few weeks, and got to know their characters, you will be able to tell straight away if all is not well, even if you cannot quite put your finger on what it is. Some signs are more obvious than others but the main ones to look out for are the following (as long as you are checking your pigs daily, as is recommended, you should be able to deal with any minor medical problems promptly and appropriately):

- wounds;
- rapid breathing;
- coughing;
- looking miserable;
- changes in stools;
- dry, flaky, red skin;
- lameness;
- vomiting;

- standing hunched up;
- loss of appetite.

DEALING WITH MEDICAL PROBLEMS

Finding a Vet

Finding a vet that is experienced in treating traditional breeds can be quite a problem nowadays, which means that it is important to do your research before you actually need one in an emergency. Your local small-animal practice will not have a suitably experienced pig vet and even larger farm practices do not always have someone who has worked with traditional breeds. Most vets can deal with day-to-day problems but when a pig is ill and the signs of what is wrong are not so obvious, that is when they could struggle

Pigs should be checked daily for signs of any problems.

with giving the correct advice and treatment.

If you live in a suburban area, finding a pig vet will be practically impossible and you may have to go further afield to register with one. This can of course increase the amount you have to pay should you need to call one out.

Administering Injections

Vet costs can sometimes be kept down if you learn how to inject your pigs yourself. Often, when a pig is ill, it will require a course of antibiotics, which will need to be administered daily until the pig recovers. The cost of a vet coming out to do this would be prohibitive, so it is important that you learn how to do it yourself. If you are planning to attend a pig course before you keep pigs, it is worth asking to be shown how to inject, so at least you

have a general idea should the need ever arise.

Depending on the nature of your pig, injecting it could prove difficult. As it is unlikely you will have an animal crush to hold it while you carry out the procedure, you will have to devise another way of preventing it careering off with the needle stuck in its side. Some pig keepers find that injecting when the pig's head is in a bucket of feed works quite well, allowing them to carry out the job quickly and with the minimum of fuss. When injecting, try if possible to have the pig standing on concrete or some other form of hard standing. That way, if the needle drops on the ground, it will be easy to see and retrieve.

Do not forget that all licensed medicines have a 'withdrawal' period of twenty-eight days, during which time your animal should not be used for food production. By law, all medicines given to your pigs have to be

GIVING INJECTIONS

There are two ways of injecting a pig:

1 Intramuscular – injected straight into the muscle, these injections are the easiest to do. The needle should be injected approximately 5–8cm (2–3in) back from the ear, usually where the loose skin borders the taut skin. Be careful not to inject too far back as you could inject into fat rather than muscle.
2 Subcutaneous – under the skin. To inject subcutaneously, fold a piece of skin just behind the ear and insert the needle at an angle to ensure you are injecting into the skin.

Both types of injection can be quite hard to administer due to the toughness of the skin. Be prepared for this and proceed in a positive manner.

Needles should be sterile and, after use, disposed of in accordance with current 'waste' regulations.

listed in your medical records. When the animal goes to slaughter, you are required to fill in a form for the abattoir, confirming that no medicines have been given within this twenty-eight-day period.

Natural products that you might use for treating a sick animal do not have a withdrawal period, although they do still need to be recorded.

Calling out the Vet

As a novice pig keeper, it will take time to have the confidence not to panic and call out the vet every time something seems not quite right. For example, it is hard not to be concerned when your pig has gone off its food and not eaten for a couple of days. Occasionally, though, this can happen, especially if the pig is in season or it is hot. In this case, there is no point carrying on feeding it its usual ration. Tempt it instead with a different sort of food, such as fruit or vegetables. A mash mixed with molasses, for instance, can sometimes kick-start its appetite, as can bananas, which pigs love.

If your pig seems well in itself and the only symptom is loss of appetite, chances are it will start eating again within two or three days. However, you should not hesitate to call the vet if it goes on for longer than two days or you start to see other symptoms appearing. Pigs can also go lame for no apparent reason and this does not necessarily warrant calling out the vet either. Sometimes, like humans, they pull a muscle or knock themselves, and this can be quite sore to begin with, although they should be fine again after a couple of days.

Worming

Your pigs should come to you wormed, and it is worth checking with the breeder if they have to put your mind at rest. You will have no need to worm them again if you are sending them off at six months.

Sometimes, weaners will develop a cough and this is often a sign that they have worms. If no other symptoms are evident and they seem well in themselves, worm them with a suitable wormer.

Opposite page: **Weaners should come to you already wormed.**

Vaccination

Some breeders would never consider vaccinating, while others consider it a necessity. However, it is highly unlikely that you will need to vaccinate your weaners, unless you know there is a problem with a certain disease in the area and your vet advises it.

FIRST AID CUPBOARD

Although it is unlikely you will need a vast array of medicines during the short life of your pigs, you should still keep a few basics. These should be kept together in a cupboard close to the pigs, and should include the following:

Baby oil – for moisturizing the skin if it becomes dry and flaky.

Vinegar – useful for cooling a pig down if it suffers from heatstroke.

Antiseptic spray and wound powder – you will probably need this at least once during the time the pigs are with you. Prices vary, so shop around.

Thermometer – a pig's temperature can be taken by inserting a thermometer into the pig's rectum, and should read approximately 38.6 to 38.8°C (101.5 to 102°F). If it is any higher, the pig probably has a fever and antibiotics will have to be given to lower it. If it is lower than this, the pig should be kept warm using a heat lamp and blankets. If the pig is in an ark, plenty of straw should be used and a blanket or old carpet should be hung over the door to keep out draughts.

Suncream – this is only needed if you have a light-coloured pig such as a Middle White. Breeds such as the Gloucester Old Spot may also need suncream rubbed into their 'pink' bits if they are starting to get sunburn.

MINOR AILMENTS

Isolation

A sick pig should, as far as possible, be moved away from other livestock to prevent any infection spreading. Rubber gloves should be worn when handling the pig and the same clothes should not be worn when handling other livestock, especially other pigs. A tray of suitable disinfectant should be placed just outside the pen and care should be taken to step in it each time you leave the pen. Even if the pig is not considered infectious, it should still be kept away from other animals to allow it to recover in peace.

Worms

Your pigs should come to you wormed and should not need worming again before they go to the abattoir. However, if you suspect your pigs do have worms, a suitable pig wormer can be purchased from your vet. This can be given either by intramuscular injection or in food or water. Injection is best, as this guarantees that the pigs receive the correct amount.

Heatstroke

Pigs are quite susceptible to heatstroke and, during a hot summer or even a muggy day, every precaution should be taken to prevent your charges from overheating. A wallow is a must during the summer, as is housing with ventilation. If your pig pen does not offer any shade

Wallows help prevent sunstroke.

from trees, something must be rigged up to give your pigs a place in which they may lie away from the sun. Straw bedding should be taken away and replaced with a cooler bedding such as wood shavings or sawdust. Signs of heatstroke include rapid breathing, excessive salivation, trembling limbs and uncoordinated movement.

If your pigs succumb to heatstroke, their temperature must be brought down as quickly as possible. Vinegar dabbed behind the ears helps reduce the temperature, as does spraying the air around the pig with cold water and turning a fan

on. Never ever throw cold water over a hot pig, as the shock could kill it. Instead, sponge its body and head with tepid water.

Sunburn

Sunburn can be a problem if you keep light-coloured pigs such as Middle Whites or Welsh. Darker-coloured pigs very rarely suffer from it. As with humans, a high-factor suncream rubbed in well can help prevent skin damage. During a particularly hot summer, keeping light-coloured pigs inside during the hottest hours can also prevent sunburn occurring.

Diarrhoea

Diarrhoea in adult pigs is unusual. When it does occur, it is often temporary, and brought on by such factors as over-eating, worms, a change of food or too many vegetables or fruit. Occasionally, your new weaners may suffer from diarrhoea within a few days of arriving, usually as a result of the stress of moving to a new place as well as a change in food. Every effort should be made to keep the weaners quiet for the first week and to give them the food to which they are accustomed. Changes to a different brand or type of food should be made gradually. A close eye should be kept on any pig that has diarrhoea and, if it does not seem to be clearing up after a day or so, you should seek advice from your vet.

Colds and Pneumonia

Like humans, pigs can catch a cold. Depending on the severity, your pig may be completely unaffected apart from a runny nose, or it might be sluggish and off its food. If possible, keep it warm and in a ventilated shelter, give it extra bedding and, if it is unwilling to eat, try tempting it with warm mashes or some vegetables.

Pneumonia can pull a pig down very quickly and can result in death within a few hours of any symptoms showing. Signs of pneumonia are rapid breathing, coughing, a high temperature and unwillingness to eat. Veterinary assistance must be sought as quickly as possible if pneumonia is suspected.

Lice and Mange

Often, lice are brought on to the property by newcomers, so all new pigs coming on to the property should be checked thoroughly for external parasites and, if they are seen to have skin problems, should not be accepted. Lice can be seen with the naked eye, especially around the ears where they tend to group before spreading over the rest of the body. If you suspect your pig has lice, injecting it with an anti-parasitic liquid as well as washing it with an anti-parasitic wash should clear up the problem.

Mange is caused by the *Sarcaptes scabiei* mite. It is a nasty disease of the skin, causing great discomfort to the pig. Signs of mange are head shaking, redness and a crusty skin. Like lice, mange favours the head and ears. If left untreated, mange will cause the pig to lose condition and, ultimately, die.

Some natural solutions such as tea tree oil also work well in eradicating lice or mange. However, advice should be taken on its correct use when using on the skin.

Lameness

Surprisingly, lameness in a pig is a common problem, due to a variety of causes. Sometimes, however, a pig will go lame for no apparent reason and recover a day or so later with no indication as to the cause of the problem.

Some of the factors that could increase the risk of lameness are a lack of bedding and wet slippery floors in a trailer or ark. Poor skeletal structure can also contribute to lameness as can injury through fighting or being trodden on. If the pig is lame for more than a couple of days and there seems to be no reason for it, call the vet as it may be a bacterial infection that has entered the leg through a small wound.

POISONOUS PLANTS

It is rare to hear of a pig dying from eating a poisonous plant as most of them are unpalatable and are left alone. However, special care should be taken when deciding where to place the pens, especially in a garden area. Some poisonous plants will make the pig ill if digested, while others may even result in death.

Pens should be checked throughout the year and any plant growing that is considered poisonous should be pulled up and burned away from livestock, preferably before it has flowered. Ragwort in particular is considered more deadly when it has been pulled up and left drying out, so make sure that no part of the plant is left lying on the ground.

Plants such as laburnum, rhododendrons and deadly nightshade are often found growing in a garden setting and can make a pig extremely ill if eaten. In the case of the rhododendrons, it is only the leaves and flowers that are toxic; the roots are non-toxic.

Bracken is often considered poisonous to pigs, but pigs have been used to clear bracken in woods for centuries. The bracken fronds contain a toxin that induces a vitamin B deficiency, which can be fatal. It is felt though that, as long as the pigs have access to fresh water and are fed their regular feed, they should suffer no ill effects.

Keep a close eye out for poisonous plants in the pig pens.

Rhododendron can make pigs very ill if they eat it.

Acorns can also sometimes make a pig ill, due to the high tannin content in the shells. However, in some countries, pigs are fed almost entirely on acorns with no ill effects. If you are planning to keep your pigs in woodland where there are large quantities of acorns, you should if possible introduce them slowly to the acorns by restricting the area in which they can wander with electric fencing, then gradually increasing it week by week. If you make sure they always have fresh water and continue with their normal feed, you should have no problems.

CARCASS DISPOSAL

If your pig dies from an illness, the carcass must be disposed of in the correct manner. Burying it or burning it is no longer allowed in the UK. Instead, it must be collected for disposal elsewhere by a licensed person. The exception is the Isle of Wight, where carcasses may still be buried, as there are no facilities for incinerating dead animals and the cost of getting them off the island to a mainland incinerator is just too high.

CHAPTER 9

The Final Journey

CHOOSING AN ABATTOIR

Unfortunately not every pig keeper has a choice when it comes to choosing an abattoir. With the introduction of more and more government rules and regulations, many family-run abattoirs, unable to find the money needed to conform, have been forced to close down. Especially if you live in an urban area, it can be extremely difficult to find an abattoir that is reasonably close to you.

Even if you do find one that is near by, there is no guarantee that it will take pigs or that it will suit all your needs. Some of the larger abattoirs refuse to take just one or two pigs on the basis that it is not cost-effective for them. This could cause major problems for the small pig keeper if abattoirs in their area are few and far between.

There is also the problem of whether an abattoir will leave your pigs' skin on or not. Some refuse to do so, as they may not have the facilities to blanch the carcass in a scalding tank. Even if they have a tank, they may not want to put it into operation for fewer than a certain number of pigs – again, because it is not cost-effective – which could be a problem if you are only taking two. Leaving the skin on is crucial if crackling is required and it is important that you clarify whether you want it on or off before you take your pigs. If they insist on skinning and you want the skin left on for the crackling, you may have to try and find another place.

If at all possible, you should try and book your pigs into an abattoir that is no more than an hour's drive away. Try and choose a family-run one – not only will you be supporting a small local business, but it is also better for the pigs' stress levels to go to a place that is smaller and has less going on.

You should try and research prospective abattoirs before you buy your pigs, or at least quite a few weeks before it is time to take them. Once you have found one, arrange a visit to discuss any concerns you may have, and also see for yourself how things are run. Do not be embarrassed to talk about how you might feel emotionally. You will not be the first, or the last, to shed a tear when the time comes and, on the whole, abattoirs are quite understanding and may give you advice on how to cope.

Check which days and what time they book pigs in, as most small abattoirs only kill pigs on a certain day. Finally, pick up a copy of the Food Production Form, which you will need to fill in before you take the pigs.

Prices for killing vary throughout mainland UK. There can even be a difference in killing price between two local abattoirs, which can be as much as £10. If you live on

Outdoor pigs have succulence to the meat that cannot be matched by intensively reared pigs.

the Scottish Islands, prices for killing and butchering pigs at your nearest abattoir, which might even be on another island, can be quite high, so this should be taken into account when working out a budget.

LEADING UP TO THE DAY

A close eye should have been kept on the pig's weight in the last few weeks before slaughter, and the food amounts changed accordingly if the pigs were putting on too much weight.

Some traditional breed producers believe that if pigs have access to a surplus of food other than their usual diet, such as apples or beech nuts, in the last three weeks before slaughter, the meat will absorb the flavour. It will be generally sweeter and tastier, while the consumption of beech nuts will give it a slightly nutty taste. There is no scientific evidence for this theory, but it is worth giving it a try.

Book your pigs in well in advance, especially around Christmas time. Some abat-

toirs stop killing brought-in pigs leading up to Christmas, in order to concentrate on their own. If your plan is to fill the freezers for Christmas, check at the end of the summer with your chosen abattoir, and book your pigs in accordingly, even if you have only just acquired the weaners. You should know roughly when they will be ready and you can always keep them longer or send them slightly earlier if the dates do not exactly match. At least you will have made the booking well in advance.

Loading pigs the night before they travel to the abattoir is illegal, due to the amount of time they are allowed to spend in a trailer. As a result, you must load the pigs in the morning, which can be quite stressful. To help keep the stress to a minimum, you should be reasonably confident that your pigs will load without too much fuss. Therefore you have to be organized. Start getting them accustomed to the trailer at least a week or two before they go, if you can, by placing the trailer in their pen with the ramp down and with a deep bed of straw. Their natural curiosity usually

Opposite page: **Finding an abattoir in an urban area may be difficult.**

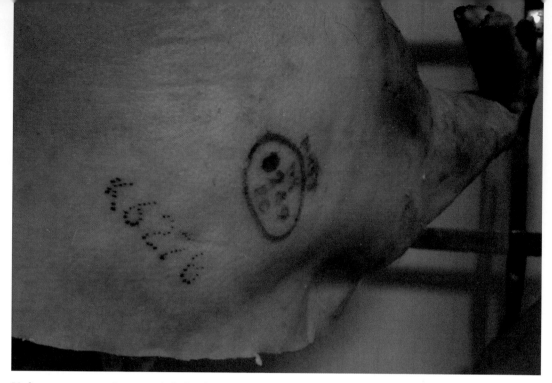

Make sure your slap-mark is legible.

gets the better of them, and you should then find that they walk in and out quite happily, especially if you feed them in the trailer as well. You may even find after a few days that they are sleeping in the trailer instead of their ark.

The person who is taking the pigs must be happy and competent in reversing the trailer and, if they are not, they must practise. Most abattoirs, if not all, require you to reverse up to the building to unload the pigs. This is usually quite straightforward, but if you go on a busy day, you will have to negotiate a number of lorries, cars and other obstacles. Spending ages trying to reverse, although it will amuse the abattoir staff greatly, will only add to what is already a stressful situation. It is definitely worth practising.

Your pigs should be tagged as well as slap-marked with your herd number a few days before. Some people tag on the day, but it does mean one more job to think about at a stressful time.

ON THE DAY

What to Expect

Most pig owners have never seen their pigs killed, because it is quite an emotionally difficult thing, taking something that you have nurtured over the past few months to its death. Many pig owners will not name their animals for this reason, as it makes them feel more connected to the animal. Others are quite happy to name them, even giving them names connected with pork.

On the whole, animals are treated with respect and with consideration as they pass through the abattoir. Many people who have never visited an abattoir often have visions of a place of terror for the unfortunate animals inside. For the majority of abattoirs, especially the smaller family-run ones, this is not true. The abattoirs themselves are clean and quiet with no obvious signs of animals waiting around and there is usually a strong smell of disinfectant rather than a smell of death.

The animals are usually dispatched quickly and, depending on the abattoir and whether they are busy or not, sometimes the pigs have been killed before you have even returned home.

Getting the Pigs to the Abattoir

Usually you will be given a time by which you need to get the pigs in. This is usually early in the morning, so you should give yourself plenty of time to load up. Even if your pigs are accustomed to the trailer, you should err on the side of caution and start loading early.

If your trailer has been left in the field, you may find your pigs are asleep in there and it is just a case of closing the ramp up and hitching up. If it has not been possible to put the trailer in the pen, you must make sure that you have enough people to help you load them in the morning. Back the trailer up to the entrance of the pen and put gates either side of the ramp to prevent the pigs escaping off the side. Using a bucket of food, encourage them slowly into the trailer. Do not rush them. The pigs will sense that you are in a hurry and, every time they back off the ramp, it will be that much harder to get them on to it again. If you feel you may have serious trouble loading them, cut back on their food rations the day before so they will be extra hungry.

Make sure when they load into the trailer that they are as clean as possible. A veterinary inspector will check them on arrival and could reject them if they are deemed to be too dirty. They will also check that the animal is well, with no obvious health issues. Ensure before leaving that you have correctly filled in all the necessary forms. Some abattoirs insist on the forms being sent over prior to dropping the animals off; check beforehand whether this is the case or not. Once you arrive, paperwork is usually handed in before the pigs are off-loaded, so the vet who is inspecting can check the paperwork against the pig. If the abattoir is also butchering your pig, you need to hand them a list of your requirements. Make sure you keep a copy so you can refer to it if there is a problem with the cuts you receive back. Sometimes, through lack of communication or just misunderstanding, mistakes can be made, so it is best to write everything down.

The emotional side of taking animals that have been part of your life for the last few months can be difficult to deal with for some people. Indeed, for a few it is too much to bear, and the pigs end up living the rest of their life with the owner rather than ending up in the freezer!

Taking your pigs for the first time to the abattoir can be extremely difficult, but you do get over it. You will find that your sense of loss will be replaced very quickly by pride when you sit down to your first home-produced joint for Sunday lunch with your family. After all, this is what raising a traditional breed is all about.

The Procedure at the Abattoir

Pigs are rendered unconscious by stunning with an electrical current using tongs to each side of the head. The pig is then shackled up by one hind leg. Once off the ground, all major blood vessels that leave the heart are cut, which produces rapid blood loss. Death happens in seconds. If the skin is being left on, the pig is then dipped in near-boiling water to loosen the bristles, before they are removed by the paddles of a de-hairing machine. The carcass is then split and disembowelment is carried out. A vet will then check that all is well with the carcass and there are no problems. Sometimes the offal is deemed unfit for human consumption and will be discarded. The owner will be given the reasons why when the pig is collected. Once checked, it is washed and chilled and hung in a cold room, awaiting collection a couple of days later.

ON RETURN

Trailers need to be disinfected within twenty-four hours of leaving the abattoir and the straw taken out and burnt. If at all possible, try to use a high-pressure hose to clean under the trailer as well as underneath the wheel arches. Some abattoirs require you to clean and disinfect the trailer before leaving their premises. If this is the case, they will inform you and show you the washing area.

A copy of your Food Production Form should be sent to your local Trading Standards in England and Wales, or Animal Health and Welfare Department if you are in Scotland. Make sure you keep a copy for your own records.

You will be told at the time of dropping the pigs off when you should come back and collect the carcass. Normally, unless the abattoir is also doing the butchering, it is two or three days later.

Traditional breeds are not suitable for intensive farming.

CHAPTER 10

The Art of Butchery

BUTCHER OR ABATTOIR?

Butchery costs can vary dramatically, so it is worth spending time looking at all your options. Most people when they first start out will ask the abattoir to butcher the meat, as many abattoirs have their own butcher on site, and this often works out cheaper in the long run. However, most abattoirs offer only the basic cutting service and maybe sausages, so, although you may save on time and money by not having to pay a butcher to collect the carcass, you might not have the range of curing and smoking services that independent butchers can offer.

Even if you are not planning now or in the future to butcher your own pigs, it pays to go on a butchery course. The different cuts of meat and the different processes are mind-boggling when you first start out. Some butchers will take advantage of your lack of understanding of the carcass, leaving you all the more confused. A butchery course will not only help you understand what the butcher is talking about, but it will also give you a greater understanding of the anatomy of the pig and the realistic quantities it is likely to yield.

MAKING ARRANGEMENTS WITH A BUTCHER

Once you are getting close to the time when your pigs will be going, you should

Ready for butchering.

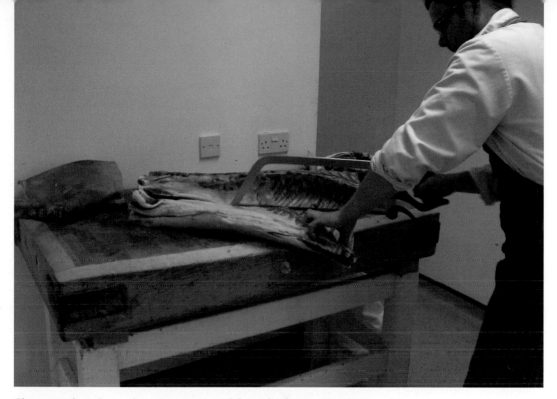

Choose a butcher who you get on with and whom you trust.

start looking for a butcher. Carcasses are not allowed by law to be collected from the abattoir in anything other than a refrigerated vehicle. Butchers local to the abattoir will therefore make some arrangement with you, for a small fee, to collect the pigs on your behalf.

Choosing an independent butcher for your precious carcasses can be a minefield and you should if possible go on recommendation.

You should not necessarily go for the cheapest butcher. You have put a lot of time and effort into your pigs so you want the best cutting service you can get. If you want smoked or cured meat, check that the butcher is able to offer this service – some cure but do not have the smoking facilities. Be aware that smoking and curing can add to the final cost considerably.

Keep it simple when using a butcher for the first time. Think about what you and your family like to eat, and do not

be persuaded to have cuts that you are unlikely ever to use. It is no good bringing belly pork home if nobody likes it and you are unlikely to want to try it in the future. Ask your butcher to make it into sausages instead. If you are asking for bacon or sausages, be clear on your preferences. You may prefer thickly sliced bacon or thin sausages, so, to avoid disappointment, make sure the butcher is aware of this.

Once you have discussed your requirements with the butcher and are happy with everything, book your pigs in. Good butchers get booked up quickly, so it is important to arrange a date that fits in with the abattoir as soon as possible.

The meat is usually hung for a couple of days before collection, to allow it to set. If this procedure has not been followed, you will end up with what is termed 'floppy pork', meat that is soft and difficult to butcher. It will be uneven in colour and also feel wet to the touch. Sometimes,

Opposite page: **Try to go on a butchery course to gain a better understanding of what is involved.**

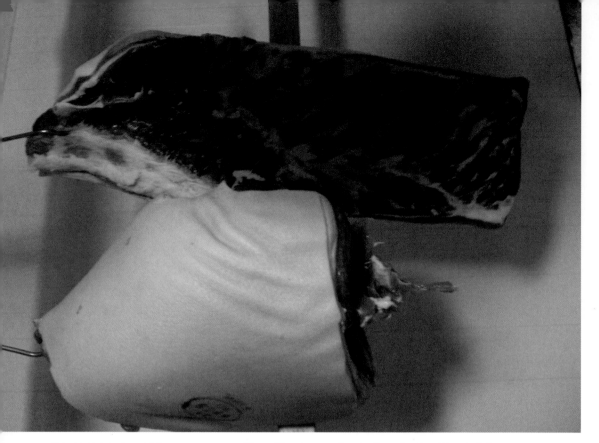

Carcasses should have no more than three-quarters of an inch of back fat.

floppy pork can be a result of the animal getting highly stressed prior to killing.

A butcher will also give you an idea as to whether your carcass has too much back fat – when producing your pigs you should be aiming for no more than three-quarters of an inch. Traditional breeds will always carry more back fat than intensively produced pigs, but too much back fat indicates that the pigs have been over-fed and that you have therefore wasted money. The butcher may also talk about the 'killing out' percentage and the lean meat percentage. The killing out percentage is the proportion of live weight of the pig that the carcass represents and will include the bones, head, skin, and so on. The lean meat percentage is the meat you get from the carcass.

BUTCHERING AT HOME

For many people, the whole process of pig keeping is not complete unless they butcher their pigs themselves. There is a certain satisfaction in producing a pig, and then butchering it. If it is not possible to attend a pig course, the next best thing is to buy a butchery DVD. Do not attempt to butcher without some knowledge of the carcass.

Cuts of Meat

The Head
Rarely used nowadays, the head is suitable for making brawn and as a base for soups and stocks.

Chaps

Technically classed as offal, chaps (also known as cheeks) are extremely tender and can be eaten hot or cold, once cooked.

Spare Rib

The spare rib is a large joint from the shoulder of the pig. It is a relatively inexpensive cut containing a large proportion of bone. However it also contains quite a fair bit of fatty connective tissue, which helps it stay moist when cooking.

Hand

A traditional roasting joint, which is often cured on the bone then boiled to make ham. It can also be cubed for casseroles or turned into sausages.

Blade

Years ago the spare rib roast was often divided into two smaller joints: the blade and the spare rib. Nowadays, this very rarely happens and sometimes the blade is removed completely.

Shoulder

The whole shoulder, comprising the spare rib, the blade and the hand, is perfect for slow roasting. The shoulder can also be used for making pork pies and salamis.

Loin

The loin produces a superb-tasting roast that can be boned and rolled as well as being left on the bone. It can be divided into three smaller joints, which can then be subdivided into chops. Curing the loin will give back bacon or, if it is kept on the bone, bacon chops.

Tenderloin

This is quite an expensive cut of meat, which can be quite difficult to cook due to its tendency to dry out. Cooked correctly, however, it is absolutely delicious.

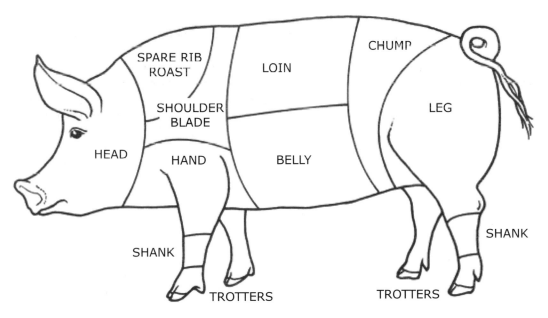

Cuts of meat and offal.

Belly

For quite a few years, belly pork was considered a poor man's dish, but it is one of the most versatile pork cuts there is. You can roast it or barbecue it, as well as curing it to make streaky bacon or pancetta. Strips of belly pork can also be cut into cubes for a casserole.

Chump

The chump is usually sold as chops or steaks. Sometimes it is also sold as a small roasting joint.

Leg

The leg of pork is the prime cut of pork, which is usually cured to make hams. Part of the leg can be made into pork steaks, while the rest is usually made into a roasting joint. High-quality bacon can also be made from the leg.

Shank

The shank is ideal for adding to soups and stews.

Trotters

Trotters are rich in flavour and are ideal for adding to stock, especially if that stock is going to be used for terrines or in pies.

Offal

You should request your offal be given back to you at the time of dropping off your pig. In some abattoirs keeping the offal is considered a perk of the job by abattoir staff and, unless you ask for it, it will mysteriously disappear. Most abattoirs if requested will give back the offal, though only after it has been given a clean bill of health.

Not all abattoirs will give you back the blood even if you ask for it. If they are happy to do so, you will have to provide a scrupulously clean bucket with a lid in which to collect it.

In the nineteenth century, some offal had uses other than being eaten. The bladder, for example, would be washed and stretched, and would then be used for poaching small game birds in.

Kidneys

Pig kidneys need to be eaten on the day of slaughter to ensure freshness, as they have a tendency to go off more quickly than calf or sheep kidneys.

Heart

Pig hearts are delicious and are ideal for stuffing.

Fries

'Fries' is the culinary term for testicles on pigs, cows and sheep. Unfortunately they are very rarely consumed in the UK because of a certain squeamishness. When marinated they are, however, extremely palatable.

Tongue

Many people do not like the idea of eating tongue, and it is rarely eaten on its own. Usually it is found in brawn.

Ears

Dried pigs' ears are often sold in pet shops for dogs to chew on. However, the usual way of preparing them for human consumption is to boil them slowly for a few hours until tender, then griddle for a few minutes until crisp.

Butchery Equipment

If you decide to do your butchering yourself, you do not need to go out and spend a small fortune on equipment. What you need will depend on what you are

Specialized equipment will be needed for burger and sausage making.

planning to do with the meat. The basic cutting equipment needed to butcher your own pig is two knives, one for boning and a large cutting knife, a saw and a board for cutting. Although it is not strictly part of the butchery equipment, you should still give thought to your freezer before you embark on butchering your pigs. Do not underestimate the amount of meat you will get from just a couple of pigs. A chest freezer measuring at least a cubic metre will be needed to hold all the meat.

If you are planning to make sausages or burgers, you will need specialist equipment. The internet is a good place to look for the appropriate items and most companies will be quite happy to advise you on what is available to suit your budget. Sometimes, you might be able to pick up equipment at discounted prices at the larger food shows and agricultural shows. Quite often, the seller will also give you a demonstration before you make any decisions to buy.

Food Regulations and Hygiene

Even when you are butchering for your own consumption and that of your family, you still have to follow regulations and hygiene guidelines.

You can no longer pick up a carcass in the back of your car even if you live just down the road from the abattoir. A carcass must be collected in a refrigerated van. If the abattoir has butchered the pig, you do not require this type of vehicle to collect the cuts of meat. Common sense dictates, however, that the meat should be transported in cool boxes.

When butchering yourself, strict measures should be put in place to minimize the risk of contamination. Hands should be washed frequently and long hair tied back. Hot water and disinfectant should be used to wash down surfaces, and windows should be kept shut to prevent flies entering your cutting area.

Meat should be frozen as soon as possible using special freezer bags and the freezer should be checked regularly to ensure the correct temperature, which is −18°C.

Butchering your own pigs will give you immense satisfaction, but it is wishful thinking to imagine that the cuts will turn out exactly the way they are meant to the first time you try your hand at it. As they say, practice makes perfect.

CHAPTER 11

Home Curing and Smoking

CURING

The practice of preserving meat by curing has been around for millions of year and, even though today the refrigerator and freezer has taken away the necessity for preserving meat by this means, there is still a demand for cured meats, especially in Europe.

Curing works by covering the meat with salt to draw out the moisture that is loved by bacteria. Care has to be taken therefore when curing meat that the cure is doing its job. If the curing is done poorly, there is a risk of the meat going off. Curing should be done in the winter months rather than the summer. If this is not possible, everything, including the room in which the meat is being processed, should be kept as cool as possible. Once the meat has been rinsed at the end of the curing period and hung up to dry, special attention should be paid to the temperature of the room to ensure it is kept cold enough.

There is no doubt that you will derive great pleasure from sitting down to a home-produced joint of pork. The satisfaction of eating your own cured or smoked pork is, however, immeasurable and to raise a couple of pigs without curing at least some part of them would certainly be regrettable.

Dry-Curing Meat

There are only four things you need to cure meat: salt (lots of it), air, time and patience. It is a relatively simple process, yet most people somehow never get around to it, even if they like the idea of it. Any cut of meat can be cured, although obviously some will take better than others. Once you have started, you will soon gain enough confidence to experiment and, even if it does not turn out as well as you hoped, it will be fun trying.

Most parts of a pig will at some time or another have been cured. In some parts of Europe, even the tails and trotters have been cured by salting, and have been added to regional dishes along with other ingredients.

Dry-curing involves applying salt to meat and then keeping it in salt for anything from five days to six weeks, depending on what you are salting.

Most people first try their hand at curing bacon as this seems less daunting. The meat must be completely fresh when it is cured; preferably it should be done as soon as the pig comes back from the abattoir. Both skinned and the scalded carcasses can be used for curing bacon.

Curing Ingredients
Salt is of course the primary ingredient. Sugar, either brown or white, is also added

to offset some of the harshness of the salt. Bacon without sugar can be too salty for most palates but it is worth experimenting with different ratios of sugar and salt until you find one that works for you. A 50/50 mix of salt and sugar seems to work best. You can cheat and buy commercially prepared cures, but you will gain more satisfaction from doing everything yourself from scratch. If your bacon turns out salty, soak in ice-cold water for four to six hours. Pat dry and hang as usual.

Once you have made a mix that gives you the flavour you require, write it down as it is very easy to forget it, especially if you are only keeping a couple of pigs every now and again.

Dry-Curing Step by Step

1 Cut your belly pork, or whichever cut you fancy, into slices and put the slices on to a tray or a large plate.
2 Weigh out the required salt, approximately 3 level teaspoons if you want it to taste like bacon, and add the sugar.
3 Rub the mix into the meat on both sides every evening for a week.
4 At the end of the week, give the bacon a thorough rinsing and hang it somewhere cool to dry.
5 Once the meat has been cured, it is ready for smoking if you desire.

Wet-Curing

Wet-curing has had some bad press in recent years; however, wet-curing in the traditional manner – submerging the meat in brine, sometimes with some herbs added – is a perfectly acceptable way of curing at home and should not be thought of as inferior. Unfortunately, in pursuit of profit, some producers have used a method of injecting artificially flavoured brine straight into the meat. Injecting meat in this way not only gives it a false appearance of being pumped-up and moist, but actually adds weight to the meat, resulting in the customer paying for water rather than meat. Bacon 'cured' in this way will leave a tell-tale scum at the bottom of the frying pan and shrink to half its size during cooking.

Air-Drying

Many specialist hams are air-dried, using a process that does not cure in the curing sense, as the meat would have already been cured by salt. Instead, it allows the meat to continue to mature and, in doing so, the flavours of the meat along with any added herbs will intensify. Many experts will tell you that it is impossible to air-dry in the UK because of the climate. However, it is still possible to make an adequate ham as long as care is taken in the hanging.

SMOKING

Smoking has been used to preserve food since recorded history began and is still popular today, although not necessarily for preserving foods, more for flavouring. In less developed countries, however, smoking to preserve food is still common. Smoking on its own, even hot smoking, is not enough to preserve, so meat must be cured before it is smoked.

All meat must be dry before any attempt at smoking, otherwise the meat will not taste as good and the smoking will not be as even. Once you have applied the smoke, it will take approximately thirty-six to forty-eight hours to complete if it is hot-smoked and much longer if you are cold-smoking. During that time you will have to top up the wood or sawdust as needed.

Although other fuels can be used for smoking, wood is by far the most popular.

Opposite page: **The Tamworth is one of the best bacon pigs you can buy.**

The type of wood you use is entirely up to you. In the UK, most people use oak; in Europe, alder and beech remain the traditional smoking wood, while in North America, the wood from the mesquite oak and the pecan, alder and maple are all used, depending on the flavour required. Fruit woods such as cherry and apple are also used, to a lesser extent.

Ideally, you need some form of smoker to smoke your meat, although it is possible to smoke over an open fire. Many farms traditionally had a smoker where meat could be smoked and stored. Nowadays, with smokers less in demand than they once were, many traditional smokehouses have fallen into disrepair.

Cold-Smoking

Temperature

The cold-smoking method is usually used to smoke 'fatty' foods such as hams and sausages. After smoking, the food is still raw but has turned a beautiful dark-red colour. The temperature of a cold-smoker should not be above 30°C centigrade, as that is the point at which the proteins start to change. To test the temperature of the smoker, place a piece of cheese on a rack at the bottom of the smoker. If it melts and starts to slide through the rack, the temperature is too high.

Method

Hang or lay the pork in the smoker. Strong clothes hangers will do for this job if you do not have anything more suitable.

Once you have got the fire going, it should be shut down to produce moist cool smoke that will infuse with the pork, and help it to lose further moisture. Up to a further 5 per cent weight loss can occur during smoking. Cold-smoking pork is a longer process than hot-smoking and

something like a ham can take weeks to complete.

Hot-Smoking

The ideal temperature for hot-smoking is usually between 74 and 85°C. If it is any higher than this, the meat will shrink. Unlike cold-smoking, which leaves the food quite dense, hot-smoking makes the meat less dense and softer.

Once the smoking process has been completed, the pork is safe to eat without further cooking.

Building a Basic Smoker

The best smokers are made of either brick or stone, since both materials hold the heat exceptionally well. However, if you have neither the inclination nor the time to build one, there are numerous other smokers on the market at various prices that

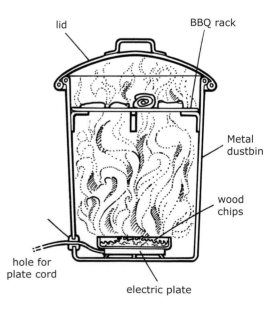

A basic smoker can be adapted from a metal dustbin.

will do an adequate job. If you are planning to do a lot of smoking, it is worthwhile investing in one; however, until you decide smoking is definitely for you, it is relatively easy to make one. You can make a basic smoker out of many things; one good base is a metal dustbin.

Buy a metal dustbin with a lid, and an electric hot plate (both of these can be purchased at hardware shops). Place the electric plate at the bottom of the bin and cut a hole in the side of the bin at the bottom, to enable you to slip the cord of the hot plate through. File down any rough edges around the hole to prevent the cord being cut.

Find a small metal box to hold the wood chips in, or, if you are any good at metalwork, make one. Put your wood chips in the metal box and place on top of the plate. Switch the plate on and in a few minutes the chips should start to burn.

Place a barbecue rack at the top on which to lay your pork. Replace the lid on the bin and leave. Check the chips regularly and replace them when necessary.

It is a good idea also to buy a temperature gauge to enable you to keep an eye on the temperature of the smoker.

CHAPTER 12

Sausage Making

HISTORY

For over nine thousand years man has been eating sausages. Unlike other foods that have been lost over the centuries, the humble sausage has gone from strength to strength. Today, there are countless types all over the world, with more than 400 regional varieties found in the UK alone. Sausages have been developed over the centuries, according to the availability of meat and spices available locally. Climate has also played a part in the type of sausage produced in a particular area. Some climates proved unsuitable for curing dried sausages so alternatives had to be found instead.

Sausages have not always been a favourite food. In AD320, Roman Emperor Constantinus I, along with the Catholic

Sausages have been around for over nine thousand years.

Church, banned people from eating them because of a connection with pagan festivals.

It was during the reign of Charles I that sausages were divided for the first time into the links that are familiar today.

During the Second World War, sausages were often referred to as 'bangers' because of their tendency to explode during cooking, due to the amount of water used in them. Steam would be produced and would break through the skin making a loud bang as it did so. The dish 'bangers and mash' still uses the name to this day.

SAUSAGE VARIATIONS

Cumberland sausage: a meaty, chunky, coarse-cut sausage. Heavy in black pepper, normally sold in lengths rather than links.

Breakfast sausage: a mildly spicy sausage that is thicker than the normal sausage.

Beef sausage: popular in Scotland.

Chorizo: a spicy sausage from Spain made with pork, red pepper and paprika. Smoked or unsmoked.

Boerewors: the South African 'farmer's sausage', of which there are many varieties. Usually made with beef and pork fat with a touch of coriander and vinegar. Can be made with other meats as well.

Bratwurst: made with pork or veal and, like the Cumberland, normally sold long.

Gloucester: made using meat from the Gloucester Old Spot pig and flavoured with sage.

Gluten-free sausage: made without cereals, aimed at people who have a wheat intolerance (coeliacs). Can be made either by using no binder and 100 per cent meat or using rice flour as the binder.

Cotechino and Zampone: traditionally used in boliito misto, these traditional boiling sausages are often served with lentils. Zampone is made from a stuffed pig's trotter.

Pork and leek: popular in Wales, where ginger is sometimes also added. Pork and chive also work well.

Lamb sausage: also made in Wales, a fatty sausage made using leek, mint or rosemary.

Italian sausage: spicy sausage made with 100 per cent meat and flavoured with pepper, fennel and chilli beans.

Lincolnshire sausage: traditional regional herb sausage made with pork, bread and sage and sometimes thyme.

Lorne: Scottish square slicing sausage. Made with beef and pork, it has a smooth texture and can be eaten in a sandwich or at breakfast. Popular in Scottish cafés.

Merguez: spicy, red sausage from North Africa, made with either beef or lamb and flavoured a hot chilli paste. Usually served with couscous.

Oxford: regional sausage made with pork, veal and lemon, and sage, savory and marjoram.

Pork and apple: made in the West Country from the meat of the Gloucester Old Spot pig. Extremely moist sausage due to the cider that is used.

Suffolk: a coarse chopped sausage with herbs.

Tomato: a distinctive red sausage using pork, tomato and basil. Popular in the Midlands.

Toulouse: a firm, meaty French sausage using coarse chopped pork, parsley, garlic and red wine.

Venison sausages: from the deer, usually made with red wine, garlic and juniper berries. Low in fat.

Wild boar: a dark, gamey sausage, sometimes using apples, red wine and garlic.

SHOP-BOUGHT VERSUS HOME-MADE

The first time you sit down to a meal containing sausages you have made yourself will be an exciting event. Even if they do not turn out just right at first, no one will notice. They will be too busy enthusing about the fact that they are eating home-made sausages from a home-produced pig.

Sausages made at home are always going to be more expensive than the cheap versions that are available in the supermarket, because of the difference in quality and ingredients. Some of the cheaper supermarket sausages have as little as 40 per cent meat in them and are bulked out with water and rusk. Most have E numbers in them, not only to extend their shelf life but also to act as thickeners, stabilizers and emulsifiers. Other E numbers also act as colour enhancers. Even the more expensive sausages can contain ingredients that you would not wish to enter your body. Buying cheap sausages nowadays can be akin to buying a cocktail of chemicals.

GETTING STARTED

Making sausages is easy once you get the hang of it, although it does help if you see how it is done first. To begin with, it is a good idea to buy some meat from the butcher and have a practice. That way you will be much more confident when embarking on the real thing using your own meat.

Equipment

Buying loads of specialized equipment is not necessary. Most of the equipment needed is usually found in the kitchen. Some equipment, such as a grinder, will of course make your life easier, but others, such as knives, you will no doubt already have, especially if you have butchered the pig yourself.

The following basic equipment will be enough to get you started:

Scales – most if not all kitchens have these.

Knives – knives you have in your kitchen will be suitable.

Grinder – the basic grinder that fits on the edge of a table can be picked up very cheaply and most kitchen shops stock them. Inside are grinding plates that grind your meat to the required consistency. These can be removed and the grinder can then be used to stuff your casings.

Stuffer – it is not necessary to buy a stuffer if you are planning simply to roll your sausages into the required length to make skinless sausages (although a sausage with no casing will tend to fall apart). Caul (a fatty membrane connecting the organs together in the pig's body), is sometimes used to wrap around sausages made in this way, resulting in a beautifully moist sausage.

Casings

Casings are the skins into which sausages are stuffed and are either man-made or natural. If you want to keep your sausages as natural as possible, then obviously natural casings should be used. Natural casings come from the intestines of pigs, sheep and cattle, and usually come in different sizes. After cleaning, they are washed in brine and packed in salt to preserve them,

Opposite page: **Home-made sausages will have the freshest of ingredients in them.**

after which they are bundled up and placed in a tub of salt and sold.

Natural casings need to be thoroughly washed and soaked before use. Not only do you need to wash out all the salt but you also need to remove the smell, which is quite pungent.

Man-made casings need little preparation when used. When you buy them, they have usually been rolled in a tube and then vacuum-packed.

Other Ingredients

Water

Water is necessary to add succulence to the meat, as well as making the meat easier to stuff into the casing.

Fat

Although you are not aiming for overly fatty sausages, some fat is necessary to help the cooking process and also help the taste.

Salt

Salt acts as a preservative but should be kept to a minimum.

Bindings

Usually made from rusk, breadcrumbs or cereal, bindings are important to hold the sausage together. Many of the cheaper sausages contain a high percentage of binding. Ideally, the binding should consist of no more than 10 to 15 per cent of the sausage.

A SIMPLE SAUSAGE

Unless you are making something quite exotic, a sausage requires very few ingredients. Below is a menu for a basic sausage.

Ingredients
1.25 sausage casings
1kg lean pork shoulder
1 tsp salt
Half a teaspoon finely ground black
    pepper
200g rusk or breadcrumbs
Equipment
Casings
Grinder
Sausage stuffer
Tray to collect the sausages

Method
1 Make sure all your equipment has been sterilized.
2 Wash and soak your casings for at least half an hour. Rinse the skins with running water.
3 Cut your meat into approximately 2 cm cubes and grind. If necessary, grind a couple of times until you have the required consistency.
4 Add the other ingredients and mix well together. You are now ready to stuff the casing.
5 Wet the end of the stuffer, or whatever you will be using, and place the end of a prepared casing over it.
6 You will need to regulate the flow of sausage into the casing. If you allow too much through, the casing will burst. As the sausage comes off the stuffer, tie the ends at regular intervals, or make links by twisting the sausage.
7 Place the sausages in the refrigerator on a tray for a few hours before freezing.
8 To finish, thoroughly wash all your equipment with hot soapy water ready for the next time, and clean down all the surfaces.

Opposite page: Casings should not be over-filled.

CHAPTER 13

Specialist Meats

HISTORY

Curing meat is not difficult. Although it is unlikely you will ever be able to match the superb taste of the Iberian ham, it is still possible to make an acceptable version of Parma ham or salami at home. Many people find the idea of curing their own meat quite daunting in the beginning, but, if you have the time and a place to hang it, such as a garage or cellar, it is definitely worth having a go. Some breeds such as the Saddleback and the Mangalitza are better for curing than other breeds. Clearly, if this is something that you are planning to do with your meat, you should bear this in mind when choosing the breed.

The processing of specialist hams and salamis is an ancient tradition that goes back thousands of years. As early as 100 BC, writers made reference to the extraordinary flavour of the air-cured ham produced around the town of Parma in Italy. Even earlier, salted preserved pork legs in the Etruscan Po River valley were traded with the rest of Italy and Greece.

The preserving of meat to make salamis is a relative newcomer when compared with Parma ham. It is believed that the process of fermenting sausage was first followed in the Mediterranean region more than 2,000 years ago and became the method of preserving meat for both the Romans and the Greeks.

IBERIAN HAM

One of the best-known pigs for specialist hams is the Iberian, found in Spain. Iberian ham is renowned throughout the world for its superb taste and quality and this is largely due to the type of food the pigs eat. From October to nearly April, in a period called the *montanera*, the Iberian pigs are taken to areas where each animal will consume over twenty thousand acorns a day, first from the Spanish oak, then, later in the season, from the gall oak and the cork oak.

The curing process can take anything up eighteen months and in that time the ham will change colour to a deep red and take on the smell of cured meat.

PARMA HAM

The Traditional Version

Parma ham is traditionally made in a relatively small area in the Province of Parma, bounded by a line that begins 5km south of the via Emilia, and runs to the shores of the Ena River in the east and to the Sitrone River in the west. Production of the hams is strictly controlled, beginning with the raising of the pigs. They must be either Landraces or Durocs and fed on a calcium-rich diet, which quite often includes whey,

The Mangalitza is an ideal breed for Parma-style ham.

a by-product of cheese. Each pig is tat-tooed with the breeder's code and the date of its birth.

Once the pigs have been slaughtered, the hams are sent to the curing houses weighing between 12 and 14kg (25–30lb), where they are analysed to check that they contain no chemical substances. After this, the hams are trimmed to maintain the tra-ditional 'chicken-leg' shape, before being stamped with the date of their arrival.

The hams are tested many times over the next eighteen months to two years before they are branded with the Ducal Crown, a symbol of guaranteed quality.

Making Parma-Style Ham at Home

When curing meat, fat composition is essen-tial. Polyunsaturated fats will go rancid and turn yellow, making them unsuitable for air curing, whereas monounsaturated fats do not spoil quickly. Mangalitzas, and other unimproved breeds such as Saddlebacks and Tamworths, tend to pro-duce more monounsaturated fats than modern breeds.

Cut the leg of pork as long as possible. You can cure the full leg, with bone in and hoof on, but for beginners it is much less risky to bone the leg prior to curing. With the bone removed, there is less chance of the meat deteriorating during the proc-ess. It is also recommended that Parma ham is made during the winter months, as the meat can more easily go off in the summer.

Ingredients
1 leg of pork
5kg (11lb) of cooking salt

1 tablespoon cracked coriander seeds
1 tablespoon cracked black pepper
White wine vinegar

Method
To bone the leg, slit through the skin with a very sharp knife all the way to the bone. Do this on the inside of the leg, where there is less meat. Carefully cut along both sides of the bone, and then underneath the bone, until you can lift the whole bone out.

Take a handful of salt and rub it in to the meat where the bone has been removed. Ensure that all the inside of the meat has a good rub, and salt covers the inside surface.

Re-form the shape of the ham, then use a sharp skewer to pierce the skin and stitch the leg back together using good-quality butcher's string. Ensure the stitches are tight; this can be a bit fiddly the first time.

Weigh the leg and make a note of the weight.

Pour 2cm (about an inch) of salt into a large container (a wine box, or other plastic box will do). Sprinkle the coriander and pepper over the salt. Place the meat on top, meat or stitches side down. Evenly pour in the rest of the salt until the leg is covered by at least 2cm of salt.

Cover with a piece of plastic or wood that just fits inside your box. Put a weight on the board – the weight needs to weigh

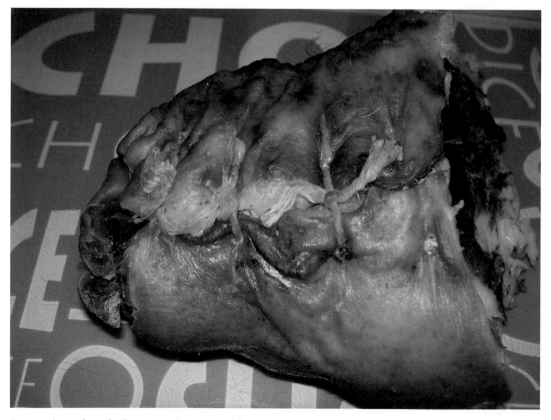

Parma ham is relative easy to cure at home.

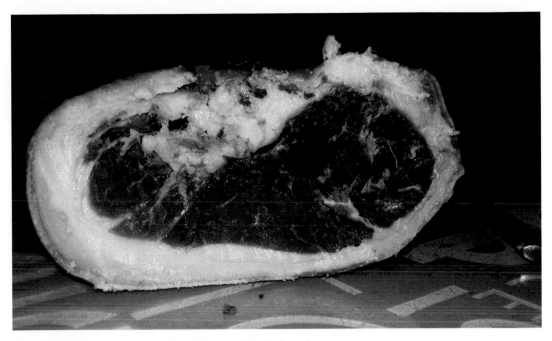

The finished cured meat should be a rich dark colour.

around twice as much as the leg. House bricks or concrete blocks work really well. Leave the box in a cool, dry place such as a garage, larder or cellar.

Leave the ham in the box for four days per kilo. When the ham has been in the box for the allotted time, remove it and wash roughly with cold water, to remove the excess salt.

Rub the joint with white wine vinegar, then wrap it in a double thickness of muslin. (If you cannot get muslin, use an old clean pillowcase instead.) Hang the ham in a cool draughty place, such as a barn, garage or porch, ensuring that there is a good airflow for ventilation and that the ham is protected from rain.

Leave the ham for four to six months until it has air-dried. When it is ready, serve it with wine or melon.

SALAMIS

The Traditional Version

Traditional salami can be made with a variety of meats, such as pork, beef, venison, lamb and goat, with additional ingredients such as wine, herbs or vinegar added for preference. All types should be well compacted with a red/pink interior speckled with fine marbling of white fat.

The mixture is left for a day to ferment, after which it is stuffed into either natural or man-made casings and hung to cure. Natural casings are often treated with an edible mould to add flavour and prevent spoiling during the curing process.

Salami comes in fresh, cooked or dry-cured varieties. It is the dry-cured salami that is so popular and often seen hanging in delicatessens, especially in Europe. This variety can be sliced and eaten straight away, unlike the fresh, which must be cooked.

Many salamis are named after the region or country where they originated, like the Hungarian and the Milano salamis. Most are flavoured with garlic while others have spices such as cinnamon in them. By law a small amount of preservatives can be used, but only in restricted amounts. Varieties are also differentiated by the coarseness of the chopped meat and the type of meat consistency, as well as the style of the casing used.

Many varieties of Italian salami have been given special Designation of Origin, which guarantees that a particular food product is made in its native geographical region using traditional methods.

Different Types of Salami

Salame di Felino
Comes from the region around Parma. It has an uneven shape with one end being smaller than the other.

Napoletano
This is a spicy salami, red in colour and similar to pepperoni. Made with lean pork and a small amount of fat, it is unlike other salamis in that it is just folded and tied at each end. Napoletano is dried for at least six months.

Finocchiona
Approximately 25cm (10in) long and made with finely ground pork and fat, with a generous use of fennel seeds in its spice mix. Usually served in thick slices.

Soppressata
Made from lean meat from the head of a pig and coarsely ground. The meat is then mixed with back fat, pepper, spices and wine. It is flattened and knotted horizontally, forming several square sections before it undergoes a forty-day ageing cycle. Usually sliced thinly by hand.

Cacciatora
This salami is regulated by region, ingredients and dimensions. Produced all over Italy, it is recognizable by its small size. Weighing less than 300g (12oz) and no longer than 20cm (8in), it was traditionally carried by hunters over their shoulder.

CHAPTER 14

Land Management and Recovery

THE PIG AS A TOOL

Within the last few years, there has been an increase in the use of pigs as a tool in managing forests and moorland. Even for the smallholder with an acre of land, pigs have proved to be extremely useful in preparing the ground for a vegetable garden or for planting.

Extensive research has been carried out on the impact of pigs on a variety of habitats including woodland, moorland and coppiced woodland. Much of this research has taken place on Scottish estates, where the use of pigs in managing land is much more prevalent than in other areas of the UK. Time and time again, land managers have observed significant improvements to the habitat once pigs have been on it.

Attacking the vegetation with gusto.

Electric fencing is useful when rotating pigs around your land.

Not all land will benefit from pigs to the same extent. Pigs can be choosy and will not always dig up what you want, nor will they always leave alone plants that should be there. The land should be checked beforehand for any flowers or plants that are protected and, if any are found, they should be fenced off. Do give the idea careful consideration before putting pigs in an area that requires clearing.

TIME RESTRAINTS

You also need to be realistic. If you are just keeping a couple of porkers, you must accept that their ability to clear a large amount of land in the short time you have them will be limited. It also depends on what plants you are hoping to clear. Rushes, for example, do not seem to interest many pigs. In most cases they will be left alone, unless the pigs have been on the same ground for months and have rooted everything else up.

Soft ground will always be turned over more quickly than ground that is rock hard, although very wet ground is not ideal for keeping a couple of pigs. The structure of the soil will be damaged very early on if pigs are continually rooting on a small area of wet ground, and young saplings and seeds could be prevented from becoming established if this continues for too long. Many breeders bring their pigs in during the winter to avoid their land turning into a quagmire. In an urban setting, you should keep pigs during the summer months for this reason.

If you have your heart set on clearing a couple of acres and have limited time in which to do it, you will either have to look at buying older pigs, preferably something like a Tamworth, which is one of the best breeds there is for rooting, or resign yourself to clearing a smaller patch of land.

You should also be aware that, once the land has been cleared, it does not necessarily mean that the weeds, bracken, and so on, will not grow back. If they do, however, they should have less vigour than before.

WHICH PIGS?

When looking to clear land, you should take into account the age of the pigs that will be living there. Land that is holding young trees or plants such as bluebells is more at risk of being damaged by older pigs than younger ones. Older pigs will bulldoze their way through almost anything, while younger pigs seem much more

Pigs can reduce grassy paddocks to bare earth in a very short time.

The land is now ready for planting or ploughing.

in control and selective about what they are eating.

Some breeds more than others will spend every moment rooting – and this is not just a gentle turning-over of the soil, but seemingly a digging down to Australia. All breeds root, especially if they are on fresh grassy ground. As a rule of thumb, pigs with turned-up noses such as the Middle White tend not to root to the same extent. If you want some hard-core rooting, employ Tamworths, and if you want a less aggressive approach, buy Middle Whites.

CONTROLLING THE CLEARANCE

Unless you are keeping your pigs on less than an acre, you should try to rotate them once it has been cleared, to allow for re-growth of young saplings and wild flowers. Pigs do not always clear what you want them to clear and there is often no rhyme or reason to it. To encourage them to root up a particular area, pig rolls should be thrown over that area. Obviously, this cannot be done if it is muddy. A close eye should be kept on the situation so that the pigs are encouraged to work their way across any patch requiring their attention.

You also have to be aware that some steep hills require bracken and such-like actually to hold the soil together, and in this case you should not aim for total clearance.

Unfortunately, when pigs clear the land, they also root up stones, from thousands of little pebbles to fairly large lumps of rock. This should be borne in mind if you are hoping to plant seeds. A vegetable garden with hundreds of stones on the surface makes life very difficult and you will probably have to clear it first before planting. This can be a time-consuming job if you live in a particularly stony area.

AFTER ROOTING

Your land will have been fertilized during the time the pigs were on it. On average, a piglet will produce 3.4kg (7–8lb) of manure a day while a one-year-old will produce around 12.5kg (27lb) a day. Pig manure has a very high nutrient content and is rich in potash and phosphorus. It is exceptionally good for root crops such as potatoes, leeks or carrots. If you are planning to turn the land back to pasture, a good seed to use is a clover mix, but take advice from your local merchant before planting.

CHAPTER 15

Recipes

Among the thousands of recipes available today, perhaps the best are the traditional ones that have survived through the centuries. Below are a few adapted recipes, some using the more unusual parts of the pig, some going back to Elizabethan and First World War times, and some that are regional to other countries. Some are easy and take just a short while to prepare and cook, whilst others are a bit more complicated. Most of these recipes cater for four to six people.

FLASKFILE MED VITLOCK OCH HONUNG (SWEDISH PORK MEAT WITH GARLIC AND HONEY)

Ingredients
500g (just over 1lb) of cubed shoulder meat
1 leek, chopped
Tablespoon of honey
Cornflour, mixed with 1 tablespoon of water

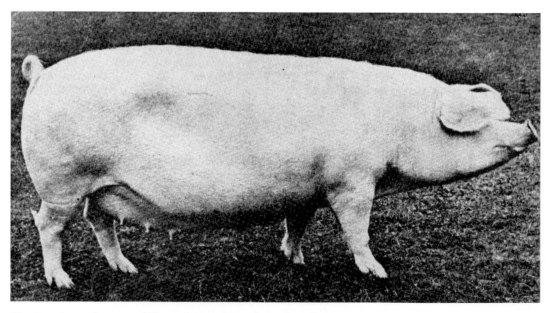

The Landrace is one of the primary breeds in Sweden.

Marinade
Half a dessertspoon of red wine
2 tablespoons of soya
2 cloves of garlic
1 teaspoon of sugar

Method
Blend the marinade ingredients together and then leave the pork in the marinade for approximately thirty minutes.

Heat a tablespoon of oil. Place the marinated pork in the pan and cook until most of the liquid has evaporated.

Add chopped leek, honey, and cornflour mixed with a tablespoon of water. Cook for two minutes and serve with rice.

FAGGOTS (THE CHEAT'S WAY)

Ingredients
Lungs and heart (tubes discarded), two-thirds lungs, one-third heart
Belly pork
Large packet of sage and onion stuffing

Method
Pre-heat the oven to 180°C centigrade (350–375°F/Gas Mark 4–5).

Chop the lungs and heart and grind the belly pork. Mix together with stuffing and roll into balls.

Bake in the oven until cooked right the way through, around 15–20 minutes.

Make up onion gravy and cover the faggots with it.

HAM AND SAGE PANCAKES

Ingredients
Cupful minced ham
2 cupfuls stale breadcrumbs
2 eggs

Pepper
Cupful scalded milk
Teaspoon of sage

Method
Mix the ham, crumbs, milk, sage and beaten eggs. Slowly drop spoonfuls into a hot buttered frying pan, and cook until brown.

SALTED PIG'S EARS

Once you have received the ears back from the abattoir, you will need to pack them in salt for approximately a week before using.

Ingredients
4 salted pig's ears
2 cups water
1 cup cider vinegar
Half a cup of the water in which the salted ears were boiled
2 onions, finely sliced
3 cloves garlic, finely sliced
1 tablespoon black pepper
5 to 6 whole allspice
4 to 5 juniper berries
10 cloves, whole
1 bay leaf

Method
Prepare the ears by salting. Boil until tender, but be careful not to over-boil. Take the ears out of the water and let them cool off. Measure half a cup of water from the pan used to boil the ears and put aside, then cut the ears into strips.

In a large glass bowl, mix the water, vinegar, juniper berries, onion, garlic, pepper, allspice, cloves and bay leaf. Add the ears and mix well. Cover the bowl and let the preparation stand for twenty-four hours before serving.

The ears are edible, but they are generally tried by the few and rejected by many.

KIDNEY RISOTTO

Ingredients
4 pigs' kidneys, cored and diced
Teaspoon of oil and butter for frying
6 large button mushrooms, quartered
1 onion, chopped
1 mug Arborio rice
1 mug water
1 mug red wine
1 mug frozen peas
Salt and ground white pepper
Pinch of cayenne pepper
Knob of butter

Method
Fry the kidneys briefly until brown and remove to a separate dish.

In the same pan, soften the onion and then add the mushrooms, the seasoning and the cayenne, and stir fry for a couple of minutes. Add the rice and stir well to coat in all the juices in the pan, then add the wine. Boil rapidly for a minute or two then add the water. Cover and simmer for ten minutes.

Add the kidneys and the peas, stir them in gently and simmer for another minute then remove from heat, re-cover and leave to stand for a further ten minutes. The rice should now have absorbed all the juices. Add the butter, stir gently so as not to break up the rice grains, and serve in a bowl with crusty bread.

BATH CHAPS (HEAVILY CURED PIGS' CHEEKS)

Ingredients for the Cure
250g (10oz) sea salt
50g (2oz) soft brown sugar
10 black peppercorns, coarsely crushed
5 juniper berries, coarsely crushed
1 bay leaf, crumbled

Method
Mix all the cure ingredients together. Weigh each bath chap – for every 500g of weight, add 75g of the cure mix.

Rub in well. Place in a plastic container or bag with any of the cure that may have fallen off the meat as you rubbed it in. Leave in the fridge for ten days, draining off any resulting liquid once a day. Do not add more cure. Do not bring into contact with any metal, including tin foil, as this will spoil your meat.

After ten days rinse the meat well, pat dry and wrap in greaseproof paper in the fridge until required.

The chaps are ideal for dicing and melting, as a base for soups, stews and cassoulet, or crisped up as salty croutons for creamy soups such as leek and potato. They will also smoke well. Please note that this is a heavily cured meat so it needs to be cooked as suggested above, and not eaten as breakfast bacon. The seasoning for any recipes that you use them in should be adjusted accordingly. The flavour, however, is second to none.

PEA AND HAM SOUP

Ingredients
One ham hock and trotter
Enough water to cover
6 peppercorns, a bay leaf, a carrot cut in half and two sticks of celery
450g (1lb) fresh peas from the garden (frozen can also be used)
2 potatoes coated in flour and diced
Half head of Savoy cabbage, thickly sliced
1 onion, diced

Method
Pre-soak the ham hock, overnight if necessary. Place in a large pan, cover with water and add the peppercorns, bay leaf, carrot and celery. Bring to the boil and simmer gently until the meat is falling from the bones.

Soften the onion in a clean pan and strain the stock into it.

Add the meat from the bones, discarding fat and skin, the stock vegetables and the peppercorns.

Add the potatoes and peas. Just before the potatoes are soft, add the cabbage.

Simmer uncovered until the potatoes are falling apart and slightly thickening the soup. Serve with crusty bread.

CRISPY PIG'S FRY

Ingredients
800–900g (around 2lb) pig's fry (sweetbreads, heart, liver, lights, melts)
Salt
1 small onion (50g/2oz approx)
Flour for coating
Ground pepper
1 teaspoon dried sage
Fat for shallow frying

Method
Prepare the sweetbreads and the heart and remove the skin and tubes of the liver. Trim excess fat and skin off the melts. Put the fry in a saucepan with just enough water to cover it. Salt lightly.

Chop and add the onion.

Heat to boiling point, skim, reduce the heat, and simmer for thirty minutes.

Drain, dry thoroughly, and cut all the meats into thin slices.

Season the flour with salt, pepper and sage, and coat the slices lightly.

Heat the fat in a frying pan and fry the slices gently, turning once, until browned on both sides.

Serve with well-flavoured thickened gravy.

SAGE AND HERB BUTTER KIDNEYS

Ingredients
4 pig's kidneys
Melted butter or oil
Pinch of dried sage
Salt and pepper
Herb butter (home-made or shop-bought)

Method
Skin and split the kidneys lengthways without separating the halves. Remove the cores. Stick a skewer through the ends of each kidney to hold it flat. Brush the kidneys with melted butter and sprinkle with sage, salt and pepper.

Cook them kidneys, cut side first, under a high grill until sealed, then reduce the heat, and turn several times for 5–10 minutes until cooked through.

Serve with a knob of herb butter.

SAUSAGES IN BARBECUE SAUCE

Ingredients
450g (1lb) pork sausages
1–2 tablespoons oil
3 tablespoons tomato purée
2 level teaspoons made mustard

Half level-teaspoon Worcestershire sauce
1 level tablespoon honey
1 level tablespoon soya sauce

Method
Lightly prick the sausages all over and arrange in a single layer in a heatproof dish.

Blend together the oil, purée, mustard, honey and Worcestershire sauce and spread over the sausages. Leave in a cool place for at least two hours, turning occasionally.

Heat the grill to moderate. Grill the sausages in their dish, basting frequently, for about ten to fifteen minutes, or until golden brown all over.

HAM CUTLETS IN CIDER

Ingredients
4 ham cutlets
1 tablespoon prepared English mustard
1 tablespoon soft brown sugar
25g (1oz) honey
300ml (½ pint) dry cider
15g (½oz) butter
1½ tablespoons plain flour

Method
Pre-heat oven to 200°C (400°F/Gas Mark 6).

Put cutlets side by side in a large oven-proof dish. Mix mustard and sugar with some of the cider to make a smooth paste and spread over chops. Leave for thirty minutes.

Bake for fifteen minutes.

Meanwhile, put the butter, flour and remaining cider in a saucepan. Heat, whisking continuously, until the sauce thickens, boils and is smooth. Simmer for 1–2 minutes. Season to taste.

Pour the sauce over the chops. Bake

for a further fifteen minutes, until cooked through.

Serve with creamed potatoes and greens.

PEANUT HAM HOCK

Ingredients
1.1kg (2½lb) bacon hock
1 small carrot, peeled
1 small onion, skinned
1 bay leaf
2 tablespoons orange marmalade
2 tablespoons demerara sugar
2 teaspoons lemon juice
Dash of Worcestershire sauce
25g (1oz) salted peanuts, chopped

Method
Put the ham into an ovenproof casserole with the carrot, onion, bay leaf and enough water to come halfway up the joint. Cover and cook at 180°C (350–375°F/Gas Mark 4–5), for about 2 hours 15 minutes.

Remove the ham, carefully cut off the rind and score the fat.

Combine the marmalade, sugar, lemon juice and Worcestershire sauce and spread it over the meat. Put the joint into a roasting tin. Raise the oven temperature to 220°C (425–450°F/Gas Mark 7) and return the joint to the oven for a further fifteen minutes to glaze.

When the joint is glazed, sprinkle on the chopped peanuts.

ROAST PORK WITH JUNIPER BERRIES

Ingredients
2kg (4½lb) rolled shoulder with skin on
2 garlic cloves, thinly sliced
12 juniper berries, ground in pestle and

mortar with ½ teaspoon of salt and pepper
300ml (10fl oz) beef stock
150ml (5fl oz) dry white wine

Method
Pre-heat the oven to fairly hot, 190°C (350°F/Gas Mark 5).

Make small incisions all over the pork and insert the garlic cloves. Score the skin and rub in the juniper berries and seasoning. Put the meat on a rack in a roasting pan and put the pan into the oven. Roast for 2 hours to 2 hours 30 minutes, or until the meat is cooked through and tender.

Remove the pork from the pan. Wrap in foil and keep warm while you make the sauce. Pour off the fat from the roasting pan. Add the stock and wine and bring to the boil, stirring constantly. Boil for eight to ten minutes, or until the liquid has reduced and thickened slightly. Pour into a warmed sauce boat.

Arrange the pork on a warmed serving dish and serve at once, accompanied by the sauce.

SAUSAGE AND BEAN WINTER SOUP

Ingredients
200g (8oz) dried white haricot beans
2 tablespoons olive oil
100g (4oz) thick-cut bacon, cubed
2 onions, finely diced
2 cloves of garlic, crushed, peeled and chopped
2 carrots, finely diced
2 sticks of celery, finely diced
1 litre (1¾ pints) chicken stock
1 bay leaf
Salt
Freshly ground black pepper
3 spicy sausages

THE SMALL WHITE YORKSHIRE PIG.

If the meat from traditional breeds is not eaten, they will die out – like this one.

Method

Soak the beans overnight in a saucepan of cold water. The next day, drain them, rinse well and return to the pan.

Cover with water, bring to the boil and simmer for one hour. Skim off any froth that rises to the top during cooking. Drain and set aside.

Heat the oil in a large saucepan and cook the bacon for five minutes until golden. Add the onions, garlic, carrot and celery, and gently sauté for five minutes. Pour in the stock, add the bay leaf and seasoning, and stir. Add the sausages whole and simmer for twenty-five minutes with a lid on the pan.

Add the drained haricot beans and simmer for a further ten minutes. Remove the sausages, slice them and return the slices to the pan. Serve with crusty bread.

ITALIAN PARMA HAM SALAD

Ingredients

275g (11oz) tin of artichokes in oil, drained

4 small tomatoes

25g (1oz) sun-dried tomatoes, cut into strips

25g (1oz) black olives, halved and pitted

25g (1oz) Parma ham, cut into strips

1 tablespoon chopped fresh basil

French Dressing
3 tablespoons olive oil
1 tablespoon wine vinegar
1 small garlic clove, crushed
½ teaspoon Dijon mustard
1 teaspoon clear honey
Salt and pepper

Method
Drain the artichokes thoroughly, then cut them into quarters and place in a bowl. Cut each tomato into six wedges and place in the bowl with the sun-dried tomatoes, olives and Parma ham.

To make the dressing, put all the ingredients into a screw-top jar and shake vigorously until the ingredients are thoroughly blended. Pour the dressing over the salad and toss well together. Serve on individual plates and garnish with fresh basil.

POTTED HEAD

Ingredients
1 pig's head
A couple of trotters, preferably back ones, as they have a little more meat on them
1 bay leaf
A dozen juniper berries
Black pepper
Thyme
Mixed spices
1 onion
Lemon juice

Method
Cut the head and trotters into smaller pieces so that they fit in a large pan. Cover with water and add bay leaf, berries, thyme, spices and chopped onion. Simmer and for the first half an hour remove any scum that floats to the top of the pan. Simmer the contents for about four hours.

Remove the head and trotters. Mix the meat and brains together and place in a dish. Add a dash of lemon juice.

Strain the stock and then boil up until the stock has reduced. Spoon a couple of spoonfuls of the stock over the meat and then refrigerate until set.

Eat the brawn cold with apple chutney.

ELIZABETHAN PORK RECIPE

You will need a small piece of cheesecloth or muslin.

Ingredients
750g (just under 2lb) rolled loin
600ml (just over a pint) veal, chicken or lamb stock
475ml (¾ pint) dry white wine
3 bay leaves
1 nutmeg, quartered
½ teaspoon thyme
½ teaspoon rosemary
½ teaspoon oregano
1½ teaspoons salt
For the sauce
1 teaspoon mustard powder
2 tablespoons white wine vinegar

Method
Place the stock, the spices tied together in the muslin, and half the white wine into a large saucepan of water (with a tight-fitting lid) and bring to the boil. Once the mixture is boiling, add the pork roll, reduce the heat to a simmer and cook until the meat is tender (about 2½ hours).

Remove the meat from the pan and place in a large bowl. Add the remaining wine to this, as well as the strained herbs from the cooking broth. Now pour just enough of the remaining cooking broth over the meat to cover it. Set the meat aside to cool and, once cold, cover with clingfilm and place in the fridge.

The meat now needs to marinate in the liquid for a week. Turn the meat once a day so that each side faces the bottom of the bowl in sequence.

After a week, remove the pork from the marinade, dry it off, remove the cloth covering and slice into 1cm thick rounds. Place these on a dish and spoon a few tablespoons of the pickling liquid (and the herbs) over. Meanwhile, mix the mustard powder with the vinegar and spoon this over the pork too.

SAUSAGE AND SULTANA CASSEROLE

Ingredients
450g (1lb) sausages
1 large onion
50g (2oz) sultanas
1 cooking apple
Sprig of fresh thyme, oregano and
    rosemary
Stock
Salt

Method
Chop up and fry the onion. Fry the sausages. Cover with stock and add sultanas, herbs and salt.

Place in a medium oven and cook slowly for 35–40 minutes.

SPICED MIX FOR PORK

Ingredients
1 tablespoon fennel seeds
1 tablespoon cumin seeds
1 tablespoon coriander seeds
¾ tablespoon ground cinnamon
1½ teaspoons dry mustard
1½ teaspoons brown sugar

Method
Toast all the seeds in a small pan. To prevent burning, cook over a medium heat, shaking the pan occasionally. Cook for 3–5 minutes, just until the first wisp of smoke appears.

Cool to room temperature, then mix all the ingredients together and grind to a powder.

CITRUS-GLAZED PORK CHOPS

Ingredients
4 pork loin chops
Salt
4 slices canned pineapple
6 slices unpeeled lemon
6 slices unpeeled lime
¾ cup honey
½ cup orange juice

Method
Brown the chops well and place in a baking dish. Season with salt and pepper.

Add water to cover the bottom of the pan. Cover tightly and bake in a medium oven for one hour.

Remove cover and place a slice of pineapple, lemon and lime on each chop. Combine the honey with the juice from the pineapple and the orange juice. Pour the liquid over the chops, return the dish to the oven and bake uncovered for thirty minutes, basting every 5–10 minutes with the glaze.

PORK SHANK

Ingredients
2 medium pork shanks
Half an onion, peeled and diced
1 carrot, peeled and diced

Celery, chopped
Sprig of fresh rosemary .
Bay leaf
Sprig of fresh thyme
Clove of garlic, peeled and chopped
200ml (7 fl oz) dry cider
100ml (3 fl oz) meat broth
Salt and pepper to taste

Method
Pre-heat the oven to 180°C (350–375°F/
Gas Mark 4–5).

Chop the carrot, onion, celery and garlic.

Trim away fat and gristle from the shanks, and season them with salt and pepper. Heat the olive oil in an ovenproof casserole and brown the shanks, adding the rosemary and turning the shanks to brown all sides. Sprinkle half the cider over the shanks, followed by the chopped vegetables, and transfer the casserole to the oven for ten minutes.

In the meantime, rinse the other herbs and tie them into a bunch. Add it to the pot and roast the shanks for about an hour, basting them from time to time with pan drippings and broth. When the meat is tender, remove it to a serving dish, cover with a sheet of tin foil, and keep it warm.

De-glaze the pan drippings, stir the remaining cider into them, briefly thicken the sauce over a high heat, strain it, and spoon it over the shanks.

HAWAIIAN PAKKAI

Ingredients
1kg (2lb) boneless pork in 25-mm (1-in)
    cubes
2 eggs
4 teaspoons flour
¼ teaspoon salt
¼ teaspoon pepper

3 green peppers
2 medium onions
6 tablespoons fat
1 can bamboo shoots
1 cup pineapple chunks
Celery stick
Sauce
5 tablespoons cornflour
5 tablespoons soya sauce
½ cup honey
⅓ cup white wine vinegar
1 cup pineapple juice

Method
Beat together the eggs, flour, salt and pepper, and thoroughly coat the cubes of pork in the egg mixture. Brown on all sides in hot fat. Cover and cook slowly for about thirty minutes. Drain excess fat. Cut onions lengthwise and peppers in cubes the same size as the meat. Add celery and pineapple chunks to meat; cover and simmer for five minutes. Add bamboo shoots, onions and peppers and simmer covered for twenty minutes.

To make the sauce, mix together the cornflour, soya sauce, honey, vinegar and pineapple juice. Cook, stirring constantly, until clear (about two minutes). Pour over meat mixture and simmer for about five minutes. Serve with rice.

ROAST PORK WITH APRICOT SAUCE

This marinated pork loin is roasted and served with apricot sauce.

Ingredients
½ cup chicken broth
½ cup soya sauce
2 small cloves garlic, grated
2 tablespoons dry mustard
2 teaspoons thyme

Pinch of oregano
1 teaspoon ground ginger
1 pork loin suitable for 4 people
Apricot Sauce
1 jar of apricot jam
2 tablespoons dry sherry
1 tablespoon soya sauce

Method
Pre-heat oven to 160°C (325°F/Gas Mark 3).

Combine the broth, soya sauce, garlic, mustard, oregano, thyme and ginger in a large bowl and mix well. Coat the pork, and cover and place in the fridge for approximately four hours. Remove the pork and place in the oven fat side up, on a rack in a roasting pan. Roast uncovered for 2 to 2½ hours.

Allow to stand for fifteen minutes before slicing. Meanwhile, combine the sauce ingredients in a saucepan over a medium heat and heat through, stirring constantly. Pour over the sliced meat before serving with roast potatoes and vegetables.

BLACK PUDDING

Ingredients
2 litres (3½ to 4 pints) fresh pig's blood
A bundle of natural casings
50g (2oz) salt
1 teaspoon brown sugar
1 teaspoon freshly ground black pepper
½ teaspoon ground mace, coriander and cayenne pepper
500g (1¼lb) medium oatmeal, soaked overnight
500g (1¼lb) pearl barley (boiled until tender, around 40 mins) (optional)
1kg (2¼lb) pork fat (ideally back fat; less if you prefer a healthier option)
1kg (2¼lb) onions, finely chopped
500ml (18fl oz) double cream

Method
Sieve the blood into a large clean bowl or bucket and stir in the salt, sugar and spices.

Finely dice the fat, and put about a quarter of it to sweat in a large heavy stockpot that is big enough to contain all the ingredients. When the fat has run a little, add the onions and sweat very gently until soft but not coloured at all. Add the rest of the fat and sweat until the pieces are slightly translucent and more fat has run.

Stir in the oats and barley and the cream, then slowly pour in the seasoned blood, stirring all the time, until it is thoroughly incorporated. The mixture will still be quite liquid.

If you want to take a short cut, or prefer the healthy option, omit the frying of the fat stage and just fry the onions.

Filling the Casings
Take a length of casing and pull the unknotted open end over the opening of the nozzle.

Hold the casing in place with one hand and ladle the mixture into the funnel with the other. Do not over-fill, and leave a good 5–7cm (2–3in) at the top to tie a second knot in the casing.

Tie the knot and place gently on to a large plate. Stir the mixture well before each filling to make sure the fat pieces are well distributed.

Lower the puddings into cold water and bring gently to a simmer; keep some cold water near by so you can add a tablespoon or so as it starts to simmer, to avoid boiling. If at any point during the cooking the puddings float to the surface, prick them with a pin. This should prevent them bursting. When they are done, lay them on a cotton cloth to cool.

If you would rather not go to the trouble (and mess) of filling casings, pour the blood mixture into a well-oiled loaf tin and bake in a *bain marie* in a moderate oven until a skewer comes out clean. This makes an ideal slicing and frying pudding.

THE PERFECT ROAST WITH GREAT CRACKLING

The key to great crackling is to have the skin very dry prior to cooking and to start the cooking process off at a very high heat.

Score the skin of your very dry joint of pork, taking care not to cut through into the meat. Chop a handful of thyme with some salt and massage this into the cuts in the skin.

Place the meat in an oven dish in a pre-heated oven at about 220°C (425–450°F/ Gas Mark 7). After half an hour turn the oven down to 180°C for thirty minutes per 500g. At the end of the cooking time, remove the meat from the oven and cover. Allow the meat to rest for thirty minutes, to relax it, making it exceptionally tender.

ROAST SUCKLING PIG WITH STUFFING

Ingredients
One piglet (make sure that it fits in the oven!)
4 red onions
Half a bottle of red wine
Some pig kidneys
Half a loaf of stale bread
2 cloves garlic
Some sage

Method
Pre-heat the oven to 220°C (425–450°F/ Gas Mark 7).

Cook the onions until tender. Add the red wine and simmer until reduced to marmalade consistency. Add the chopped kidneys and chopped bread. Season with salt and pepper. Add the garlic and sage. Score the skin of the piglet then stuff with the mixture and close with string. Rub the piglet with salt. Place the piglet on an oven tray in the pre-heated oven and rub in oil. After thirty minutes, reduce the heat to 180°C for three to four hours, depending on the size of the pig (approximately 30 minutes per 500g – remember to weigh the pig complete with stuffing when working out cooking times).

Allow the piglet to rest after cooking, then enjoy.

PORK SHANKS IN SAUERKRAUT

As this is a very versatile recipe and can be as easily cooked for one as for ten, the ingredients have been given per shank. Allow one small shank per person or one large shank between two.

Ingredients
2 slices of bacon (diced)
200g (8oz) sauerkraut (rinsed and drained)
1 large pinch ground allspice
1 teaspoon Dijon mustard
50ml (2fl oz) beer
Salt and pepper to taste
1 small onion
1 bay leaf
1 teaspoon brown sugar

Method
Pre-heat the oven to 180°C (350–375°F/ Gas Mark 4–5).

Fry the bacon and onion until the onion is soft, then remove from the pan. Season and brown the shanks on all sides. In a bowl, mix together the remaining ingredients and add the onion and bacon. Put this mixture in the bottom of an oven dish and place the shanks on top. Cover and place in the oven for 2 to 2½ hours until the shanks are very tender.

Opposite page: **A piglet working the teat.**

Glossary

Ark Outdoor, moveable pig housing

Boar Uncastrated male pig

Boar taint A distintive smell and taste sometimes found in boar meat. Said to be found only in boars that are sexually active

Back fat Depth of fat along the back

Carcass Dressed body of the pig

Creep Small high-protein pellets given to piglets

Dished A face with an upturned snout such as the Middle White

Farrowing Giving birth

Gilt Female pig that has not yet produced a litter

Grower food High-protein food usually given to young stock

Ham Cooked gammon

Lop-eared Ears that fall over the eyes

Meal Flakes of grain such as barley, moistened and fed as a mash to the pigs

Nipple drinkers An automatic watering system activated by the pig pushing a part of the drinker

Paddle A combined slapboard and pig stick used for moving pigs

Pig oil A by-product of the petroluem industry that is used to moisten the pig's skin

Pig roll A large nut fed to adult pigs

Porker A pig that has been fattened for the freezer, usually around six months old

Prick eared A breed with ears that stand up

Rooter Some breeds tend to root up the ground more than others, such as the Tamworth

Scouring Diarrhoea

Slap board Used as an aid in conjunction with a pig stick for moving pigs

Slap-mark A form of tattoo used for identifying the carcass

Sow Female pig after farrowing

Weaner Piglet just taken from its mother, usually eight to ten weeks' old

Weight tape A specialist tape used for finding out the weight of a pig before it goes to the abattoir

Withdrawal period The time (usually 28 days) during which an animal may not be used for food production following an administration of a medicine

Useful Addresses

BRITISH PIG ASSOCIATION
Trumpington Mews, 40b High Street,
Trumpington, Cambridge CB2 9LS
Tel: 01223 845100
Fax: 01223 846235
bpa@britishpigs.org

CLUBS AND SOCIETIES

Berkshire Pig Breeders Club
Secretary: Mrs S Barnfield
The Moby, Hopes Ash Farm, Hope Mansell,
Nr Ross-on-Wye, Herefordshire HR9 5JT
Tel: 01989 750079
www.berkshirepigs.org.uk
enquiries@berkshirepigs.org.uk

British Saddleback Breeders Club
Secretary: Mr Richard Lutwyche
Dryft Cottage, South Cerney, Cirencester
Gloucestershire GL7 5UB
Tel: 01285 860229
www.saddlebacks.org.uk
mail@saddlebacks.org.uk

Gloucestershire Old Spots Breeders Club
Secretary: Mr Richard Lutwyche
Dryft Cottage, South Cerney, Cirencester
Gloucestershire GL7 5UB
Tel: 01285 860229
www.oldspots.com
info@oldspots.org.uk

Large Black Breeders Club
Secretary: Mrs Janice Wood
20 Alice Street, Sale,
Cheshire M33 3JF
Tel: 0161 976 4734
www.largeblackpigs.co.uk
kenworthyflock@fsmail.net

Middle White Breeders Club
Secretary: Mrs Miranda Squire
Benson Lodge, 50 Old Slade Lane,
Iver, Buckinghamshire SL0 9DR
Tel: 01753 654166
miranda@middlewhites.freeserve.co.uk

Oxford Sandy & Black Club
Secretary: Mrs Heather Royle
Lower Coombe Farm, Blandford Road,
Coombe Bissell, Salisbury, Wiltshire SP5 4LJ
Tel: 01722 718263
www.oxfordsandypigs.co.uk
OSBpigs@homecall.co.uk

Tamworth Breeders Club
Secretary: Carolyn MacInnes
Boundary House, Gainsborough Road,
Girton, Newark, Nottinghamshire NG23 7HX
Tel: 01205 871792
Mobile: 07771 797613
www.tamworthbreedersclub.co.uk
secretary@tamworthbreedersclub.co.uk

The Pedigree Welsh Pig Society
Secretary: Lorna Rogers
57 Cannons Gate, Clevedon, North Somerset
BS21 5HL
Tel: 07966 583896
lorni-lou@fsmail.net

The British Kune Kune Society
Secretary and Enquiries: Hannah Smith
Tel: 01348 840098
thesmiths@hannahandmike.freeserve.co.uk

L'Association British Pigs in France
Secretary: Mrs Linda Totty
www.labpif.com

Wales and Border Counties Pig Breeders Association
Chairman: Keith Brown
Trewen, Golf Links Road, Builth Wells, LD2 3NF
Tel: 01982 552100
chisholmkv@tiscali.co.uk

COURSES

Below is listed a selection of pig and butchery courses in the UK.

Bidgiemire Pig Co
Tel: 01864 505050
bidgiemire@btconnect.com
www.pig-arcs.co.uk
Day pig courses and supplier of all pig equipment in Scotland

Hidden Valley Pigs
Tel: 01598 753545
email: debbie@ilkerton.fsnet.co.uk
www.hiddenvalleypigs.co.uk
Weekend smallholder courses, butchery course and pig-keeping courses and farm shop on Exmoor

The Ginger Piggery
Tel: 01985 850381
caroline@boytonfarm.co.uk
www.thegingerpiggery.co.uk
Butchery courses and farm shop in Wiltshire

Wendy Scudamore
Barton Hill Farm
Tel: 01981 240749
wendy@bartonhill.co.uk
www.bartonhill.co.uk
Pig day courses in Herefordshire aimed at anyone planning to keep or already have Kune Kunes. Wendy's pigs are sucessful film stars in their own right

Sarah Dodds
Yearle Farm
Tel: 01668 281336 or 01668 283163
info@yearletamworths.co.uk
www.yearletamworths.co.uk
Day pig courses in Northumberland working with Tamworths

Oaklands Pigs
Tel: 01892 852663
enquiries@oaklandspigs.co.uk
www.oaklandsfarm.website.orange.co.uk
Day pig courses in the beautiful East Sussex countryside working with Saddlebacks.

River Cottage
Tel: 01297 630302
events@rivercottage.net
www.rivercottage.net
River Cottage run both courses and online courses.

Index